THE GOLDEN AGE
OF SPANISH SCULPTURE

MANUEL GÓMEZ MORENO

THE GOLDEN AGE

OF

SPANISH

SCULPTURE

NOTES ON THE PLATES BY
MARIA ELENA GÓMEZ MORENO

88 BLACK AND WHITE PHOTOGRAPHS BY
F.L. KENETT

12 COLOUR PHOTOGRAPHS BY
PAUL PIETZSCH

NEW YORK GRAPHIC SOCIETY
GREENWICH, CONNECTICUT

The publishers would like to express their thanks to the authorities of the cathedrals of Burgos, Granada, Segovia, Seville and Toledo, and the Museo de Escultura, Valladolid, and to all the institutions and individuals who have made it possible to obtain the photographs reproduced in this book.

INTRODUCTION

THE INDIVIDUAL CHARACTER AND HEIGHTENED SENSE OF PERSONALITY OF THE SPANIARD HAVE ALWAYS ATTRACTED DISCUSSION. THE SPANIARD CONSIDERS HIMSELF A KING IN HIS OWN RIGHT AND AS SOMETHING APART FROM THE COLLECTIVE MASS OF HIS FELLOW countrymen. He is sometimes led to act in ways quite beyond the comprehension of other Europeans, with the result that their mutual relationship will suffer from a certain tension and mistrust. Spain has been praised and envied for her physical characteristics and the genius of her people, but she has always been a difficult nation to evaluate correctly. The Spaniard's own reluctance to submit to guidance – except when it is clearly to his advantage to do so – has encouraged him to rely on his own initiative in many activities, and one of these is sculpture, an art that is particularly concerned with the interpretation of the individual in his entirety.

The art of sculpture attained limited perfection in the Egypt of the Pharaohs, where its transcendental aim was to immortalize the physical aspect of man, preserving it for all eternity. It then spread to ancient Greece and this development was to be of vital importance to the future history of art. The spirit of pre-classical Greece survived in the humble *tanagra* figurines, but under Pericles, sculpture exalted the physical aspect of man by selecting and idealizing certain features taken from reality, thus establishing the classical concept of beauty. When Greek sculpture spread to Rome it lost its polychromy. The classical style was revived in European art at the time of the Renaissance, but only after the interim period of the Middle Ages, when any idea that seemed 'new' was suppressed and there was a general return to simpler and more transcendental art forms.

Indeed, once Christianity had triumphed under the Emperor Constantine, both sculpture and the idolatry it had served fell under an anathema. However, in spite of everything, the urge to make plastic images survived and gradually reasserted itself throughout the barbarous Dark Ages. Sculpture became an integral part of the Christian faith and ritual and evolved a new artistic canon. Its purpose was no longer to express an idealized concept of beauty by a process of selection but rather to mirror the reality, spirit and emotions of the world around it, with the use of colour again to strengthen its power of expression. It was thus that the Spaniard responded, through his polychromatic imagery, to a heritage that was very ancient and very Christian, in contrast to the traditions of other European countries. Spanish art was the least influenced by classical antiquity and it was this that gave it its originality and its strength.

The progress of sculpture during the Middle Ages was slow and laborious. It began with the art of Byzantium, which enshrined the classical tradition while eliminating anything that smacked of idolatry. It was opposed to the representation of the nude and its sculptures were mostly reliefs embellished with precious materials, gold, silver, marble and copper, until finally the value of the finished work lay more in its materials than in its plasticity. With a few significant exceptions, the art was generally undistinguished.

In Spain the Constantinian series of sarcophagi with relief carvings are little more than imported art. Once they had lost sight of the classical tradition, Spanish sculptors were only able to produce a few stone figures and crudely attempted reliefs. They were simple in inspiration and execution, mainly consisting of scenes from the Bible or the lives of saints, and were regarded as decorative adjuncts to the Christian ritual. This style lasted from the reigns of the Visigothic kings in the seventh century, at Toledo and Cordova, San Pedro de la Nave and Quintanilla, until the reign of the Asturian kings at Naranco, Liño and Lena. In addition there was the mozarabic art of the tenth century which was almost entirely devoid of representation since the famous anti-iconographic canon of the Council of Eliberri in the fourth century had prohibited figurative work in early Spanish art. In the tenth century the Caliphate of Cordova stood outside the frontiers of the Christian kingdoms and its artistic superiority was apparent in its marble carvings inspired by the art of Byzantium. They foreshadowed the purely ornamental, but Christian, styles that spread throughout Castile, while the sudden flowering of imagery in the Roussillon, which began in 1020 and may be seen in the carved lintel of the church at San Genis les Fontes, was the result of a new wave of Byzantinism from Italy.

In the eleventh century there was a great cultural and artistic revival in western Europe. This was the beginning of the period of Romanesque art, in which Spain played a vigorous part, with the encouragement of the German empire under Otto the Great. The marvellous marble crosses of the kings Fernando and Sancho at León were carved at this time, approximately 1060. Soon the kings were sufficiently inspired by the Spanish taste for representational art to have the story of San Millán de la Cogolla carved on the Saint's reliquary. The new artistic awakening spread to metalwork and can be studied in the casket of San Isidoro of León and the Holy Ark of Oviedo, made between 1063 and 1075. At the same time a similarly inventive artistic impulse resulted in the carving of the monumental sculpture in the church of San Isidoro and Jaca Cathedral. These works surpassed anything being made in the rest of Europe – a fact that has been acknowledged even by French scholars.

During the twelfth century Spanish art kept up this style in a more exalted form. Outstanding examples are the façade of the *Platerías* and the famous *Gloria* portal at the cathedral at Santiago de Compostela, signed by Masters Esteban and Mateo respectively. In Avila, where sculpture was heavily influenced by Byzantium, the first signs of Gothic elements made their appearance in architecture. This was the dominant note in the work of Master Fruchel who had undoubtedly been trained in the Parisian style of St Denis under Abbot Suger. Master Fruchel was thus able to give a much stronger feeling of life to his figures, which were a blend of the Byzantine and the French, with all the artist's characteristic elegance and dignity. The progressive Master Mateo was his pupil.

These varied influences came together in the thirteenth century and began to make themselves felt under the banner of Gothicism. The Gothic style reached its climax in the reign of Alfonso the Wise when the great Cathedrals of Burgos and León were built in the style that Master Enrique had brought with him from Champagne. In Spain, religion became humanized and developed an increasing awareness of the visible world. Kings with their attendant noblemen were realistically represented. We can still observe them in all their sombre elegance, in reliefs that are suffused with a feeling of yearning towards the infinite and the divine. The ordinary mass of the people were no longer content to let themselves be guided through life by the austere and didactic monks, as in the Romanesque period. Society was ready to take its pleasures in a world in which there was an equal balance between the temporal and the heavenly. The new feeling made it possible for art to express spiritual values through the medium of earthly beauty and artists were encouraged to depict the world around them. It is unimportant that nearly all the artists we have mentioned came from abroad; there was no comparable stimulus in Spain and no indigenous school of art, but the attraction of foreign influences made up for these shortcomings. It has been proved more than once that there is something about the Spanish landscape, people, and character that always influences the foreigner who, like El Greco, is finally hispanicized. The result in art was that the importation of technical skill was allied to a peculiarly Spanish vitality and as the foreign artists became assimilated so their talents shone forth more brightly.

This process of assimilation came to a head in the fifteenth century, following the crisis of the fourteenth, which had been a crucial time for a society encompassed by agonizing problems and an art that declined in style and lacked ideals. In the fourteenth century there was still a great deal of sculpture, particularly in the frontier region between Navarre and Catalonia where French influence was strong, and even some outstanding works, especially altarpieces and tombs which were then a novelty, but there were no great artists or changes in style. The only exception was an abortive wave of influence from Tuscany which resulted in such rather typical figures as those for the baptistery in Tarragona Cathedral.

The fifteenth century was in complete contrast and may be taken as the prelude to our modern age for it was a time of innovation, ostentation and general broad-mindedness. It was then that Spanish commerce extended to northern Europe which, in return, sent a steady stream of artists pouring into Spain to revitalize her sculpture. First the Burgundian art of Claus Sluter was introduced by Janin Lomme from Tournai, who made the tomb for Charles the Noble at Pamplona, and by Guillén Sagrera, a more original artist. Sagrera had shown his talent in his building of the *lonja* (Exchange) at Palma de Mallorca before being called to Naples to work for Alfonso V. Next came Van Eyck's Flemish style which a certain Jusquín brought to Castile in his carvings for León Cathedral and a tomb at Siguenza dated 1426, probably by the same hand. The art of Flanders also reached Seville through Lorenzo Mercadente de Bretaña who made charming figures of typically Spanish characters dressed as saints. The style characterizing the work of the Egas brothers from Brussels, of Juan Alemán in Toledo, and of Juan de Colonia in Burgos was more Germanic. Burgos and Toledo became great centres of artistic activity after the downfall of Henry IV and the rise of the Catholic monarchs, events which were reflected in every sphere of life. The new impulse the monarchs gave to sculpture can be seen in the convent of San Juan de los Reyes, Toledo, with its plethora of imagery carved by Egas, and in the altar and tombs made by Master Gil Siloe for the Carthusian monastery at Miraflores. Sculpture had been given a new sense of purpose. Its artists infused the Gothic style with fresh life in its final period and used all its trappings to magnificent effect in their decorative compositions, their draperies carved in broken, angular lines, and the naturalistic expressions of their figures. This style is called *Isabelline* in honoured memory of the great queen. Colour made a definitive return to Spanish sculpture once wood was adopted as the material for portable images and particularly for the huge altarpieces which became a Spanish speciality. The great altar in Seville Cathedral, which was carved by Germans, is the largest in Christendom, and the one at Miraflores is the most poetical in composition.

As we now know, colour in sculpture is almost as old as carving itself and indeed was once regarded as its essential attribute. In ancient Greece colour in sculpture was taken so much for granted that Phidias and Praxiteles were deliberately breaking with tradition when they stopped using it in order to exalt the marble surface of their statues; but in the ensuing decadent period colour fell into complete disuse. But when medieval Christianity made it a principle to exclude plastic expression for fear of idolatry, colour, especially gold which suggested celestial radiance and gave a superhuman quality to statues, returned to favour. The use of gilt gradually gave way to polychromy until, in the fifteenth century, skilful painters made wooden statues almost completely naturalistic. Diego de la Cruz, working in collaboration with Master Gil, used reds and blues over a gilt ground in his altarpieces. He simulated the effect of brocaded textiles by using an engraving tool in the Flemish manner, scratching away some of the colours in order to show the gold underneath. This was the technique known as *estofado*: it became a Spanish speciality and was in use at the beginning of the period covered by this book.

While this Isabelline style was giving a completely new look to Gothic art by its originality and inventiveness, the Spanish monarchs were looking towards Italy. Among their statesmen were the Grand Cardinal of Spain, Don Pedro González de Mendoza, a member of the Order of the Holy Cross of Jerusalem, who was in Rome together with his nephew Don Iñigo López de Mendoza, Count of Tendilla, who was the Spanish Ambassador and had been acclaimed as the peacemaker of Italy in 1486. They came into contact with Roman culture and it was through them that the new classicism of the Renaissance made its way into Spain. But there, instead of arousing popular enthusiasm to justify its adoption, it clashed with Gothicism, and so deeprooted was the older style that it transmitted its spiritual content to the art forms inspired by the Renaissance.

The Italianizing process began to be felt in 1483 when the Grand Cardinal brought the Spanish painter Pedro Berruguete to Toledo to decorate the Cathedral. Berruguete had only recently returned from Italy where he had met the great masters and their influence may well account for his vigorous painting style. In 1489 he transformed the architectural decoration of the college of Santa Cruz at Valladolid. The alterations were made in the *Roman,* as the new style was called, as opposed to the Gothic which was called *modern*. He was assisted in his work by a certain Lorenzo Vázquez from Segovia, who carried out decorations in the Italian style but carved figures in harmony with the Flemish tradition.

The Count of Tendilla had founded the convent of San Antonio de Mondéjar, which is now ruined, and had it decorated in the new style. It was also probably due to the queen's influence that a sumptuous tomb was built for the Grand Cardinal in Toledo Cathedral; it was sculpted in the Florentine style as practised at Rome by Andrea Bregno, but the name of its artist is no longer known. Next, acting on his own initiative, the Count of Tendilla commissioned the Italian sculptor Domenico di Sandro Fancelli from Settignano to build another wall-tomb for his brother, the Archbishop of Seville. Fancelli was then commissioned by the king for two magnificent free-standing tombs for Prince Don Juan and the queen. These marvellous works can still be seen in their respective sites at Ávila and Granada. Although they are far from Spanish in style, they had a certain influence on Spanish artists and are certainly the finest works executed by an Italian in Spain.

Fancelli was followed by another sculptor whose last works were influenced by him, after a certain amount of vacillation between the Italian and Spanish styles due to the fact that the area where he worked was strongly in favour of the Gothic. This was Vasco de la Zarza, who had been trained in a Lombard workshop where his decorative style became influenced by a kind of exuberant pseudo-Romanism while, to a lesser degree, his figures displayed elements of the classicism that had been triumphing all over Tuscany. His first work in Spain seems to have been at Cuellar where he worked in the chapel of the Franciscan monastery founded by the famous Duke of Albuquerque, Don Beltrán de la Cueva. Here he made two great alabaster wall-tombs, now in the possession of the Hispanic Society of New York, which reveal a transition from Gothic to Italian style. The first tomb is wholly Gothic in its composition and was made for the Duke's brother, the Bishop of Palencia. The other is a completely Italian work and was made for the Duke's second wife, Doña Mencía Enríquez de Toledo, according to a provision in his will. Despite their structural differences the tombs share the same style in their figures. They are quite openly Italian in their inspiration and are carved with simplicity, elegance and realism, although they lack the discipline of form and the vigour that characterized Tuscan art.

According to documents, Zarza stayed some time in Ávila where he carved the altar for the Cathedral in 1499. The altar shows a highly successful blending of Gothic and Renaissance elements, in contrast to the decorations for the altar-screen which are entirely free from any Gothicism, and the seated effigy of the Bishop Alfonso Tostado in the centre shows traces of Fancelli's influence. The latter's style became more pronounced in Zarza's later work when he carved a large wall-tomb for the Bishop of Ávila, Don Alonso Carrillo, who had died in 1514, and his first decorations for the hospital of Santa Cruz. Zarza may also have been responsible for the building of the hospital itself, begun in 1504, for he had begun to practise architecture. He disappeared from the scene in 1524 leaving behind him several talented pupils. The discovery of this artist in recent times is of the greatest value in the difficult task of evaluating Renaissance influence in Castile.

Although the Mendozas had championed the artistic invasion from Italy it was strongly resisted by the new Bishop of Toledo, Cardinal Cisneros, who had been in opposition to his immediate predecessor. As a result a fierce battle ensued between the rival schools in 1498 when a number of artists submitted designs and models for the great altar of the Cathedral. On one side there were the Gothicists, including Master Gil Siloe and Rodrigo Alemán, and on the other stood Zarza, Felipe Vigarny de Borgoña, and a certain Andrés Florentín who may have been the famous Andrea de Sansovino who had just arrived from Portugal. Andrés Florentín was commissioned for the figure sculpture but he never returned to fulfil the contract and as a result the work was entirely Gothic in character. Its design was based on the altar at Seville, with divisions into box-like compartments to house the various biblical scenes. The sculpture lacks character and shows little of the new Italian influence except in a few posthumously added ornaments and in some of the relief figures which were probably carved from designs by Andrés Florentín, Zarza and Master Felipe. It was Master Felipe who carved the four centre reliefs in the altar, the remainder being executed with the assistance of two masters of the Gothic style. The two apostles on the evangelist side can possibly be attributed to Andrés Florentín, but, despite the latter's intervention in the work, the artist whom we must now consider as the initiator of the Spanish Renaissance is none other than Felipe de Borgoña or Vigarny. As a figure sculptor he achieved success from the time of his first appearance in Burgos until his death in 1543. His activity was immense, for we find him working almost simultaneously at Toledo, Salamanca and Palencia, then at Saragossa, from there to Granada after a brief return to Burgos, and finally at Toledo where he came into contact with Diego Siloe and Alonso Berruguete, who surpassed him artistically but not in prestige. Vigarny's first documented work after 1498 consists of three large reliefs carved for the *trasaltar* (reverse side of the altar-screen) in Burgos Cathedral. Their style is wholly that of Burgundian Gothic sculpture with a characteristic mastery of form, naturalism, and skilful grouping of figures in a composition that is highly original and quite masterly in its perfection. The only traces of the Roman style lie in the treatment of architectural perspective and in some of the armour of the figures which has classical elements. Similar characteristics of style and examples of Vigarny's talent are found in even earlier works such as the statuette of Esdras and one of the other figures for the tomb of John II at Miraflores, and a relief for the tomb of Juan de Padilla at Burgos which would suggest that he had begun working under Master Gil, the architect of the tombs. Another work which may be entirely by Vigarny's own hand is the very beautiful Gothic tomb of Doña María Manuel now in Burgos Museum. Although he began carving only in stone and alabaster, he later preferred to work in wood which was afterwards gilded and painted by another hand, to the detriment of the accomplished carving. He also carved figures for the altar at Toledo Cathedral, that at Salamanca University (only partially preserved), and Palencia Cathedral, the last designed in 1505 in the Lombard-Renaissance style by Pedro de Guadelupe. With the exception of a few graceful representations of the Virgin which stand out among the rest, most of Vigarny's series of pious figures in these altars suffer from a monotony and lack of character and are generally poor in expression. The fact is that once he had become a member of the artists' guild and had his own workshop, his own pupils, and plenty of commissions, his work declined in quality. Much of it was carried out by others in a routine manner under his supervision. Once he began to rest on his laurels his work betrayed the hands of the other artists with whom he was associating.

First to appear by his side was the enigmatic Andrés de Nájera or de San Juan who worked with him after 1506 on the choir-stalls in Burgos Cathedral. These contained two series of bas-reliefs of biblical scenes in which the carving is generally spoiled by the triviality of the compositions. Vigarny's art is seen to better advantage in some of the figures for the *guarda-polvo* (canopy) which are naturalistic and elegant. Most remarkable of all are the portrait busts in relief over the escutcheons on the backs of the seats. They are quite unashamedly classical and their Italianate ornamental motifs are in perfect harmony with the profusion of intarsia work used in clusters of fantastic figures which have not yet been illustrated. This was undoubtedly the work of Nájera, for it shows his Italian Renaissance training. An earlier example of his work in this style can be seen in the choir-stalls in Plasencia Cathedral which were completed by Rodrigo Alemán in 1497. The intarsia panels of the stalls are covered with beautiful *grotteschi*, figures of saints and portraits of the Catholic monarchs on the irrespective stalls.

By 1504 Andrés de Nájera had become esteemed for his wisdom and his skill in figure sculpture. He was still remembered in 1533 when Alonso Berruguete described him as a very noble gentleman and hoped for his appraisal of his work, but on the whole his activities remain obscure. He painted altarpieces at Soria, directed the carving of the choir-stalls in the Cathedral of Santo Domingo de la Calzada in Logroño as Master of the work, and he held a similar position in the church of San Benito at Valladolid and perhaps also that at Calahorra. In view of his masterly work in Santo Domingo in 1531 it is even possible that he also worked on the great altar which was begun in the same year. He may have been responsible for the design six years before Damián Forment was commissioned to complete it.

This altar is different from anything the great Levantine sculptor had made before. After leaving his native Valencia, Forment dominated the art of sculpture throughout Aragon. The design of his altars is Gothic and archaic but his figure sculpture is Italianate. He made his debut in 1509 in Saragossa with an imposing alabaster altarpiece for the church of El Pilar, and in 1520 he began carving the altar at Huesca Cathedral. The works are similar and the second shows no advance in style over the first. His altar for San Pablo, Saragossa is another equally conservative work, carved in unpainted wood. On the other hand, he showed a progression towards the Roman style in his altar for the monastery at Poblet, but the sculpture for this large work is without interest. Forment's figure sculpture is precise and elegant and always peaceful in character. Neither his figures nor even his large compositions arouse emotion, and his technique was always so sober that it is hard to place him with the Renaissance artists. Nonetheless, the effect produced by his great altar at Santo Domingo de la Calzada is a striking one. This is due as much to the sheer opulence of the work, with its strongly pagan ornamental figures and its sumptuous polychromy, as to the liveliness of the figures which seem to echo Berruguete's style, although Forment paid more attention than the latter to bodily structure and always gave his figures a classical balance. It would also seem that Forment's rich ornamentation was inspired by the tomb of the Viceroy Don Ramón de Cardona at Bellpuig (Catalonia) which was the work of Juan de Nola, a former follower of Ordóñez in Naples. The altar constituted a prototype for all the others, equally ostentatious, later made in the Rioja region and its surrounding districts, that at Abalos being an outstanding example.

Forment was surrounded by a flourishing group of Renaissance artists whose work was precise but unfeeling. Among the most important were Gabriel Joly from Picardy, who worked after 1515, and the Florentine Juan de Moreto whose skilful decorations are in the style of Sansovino, although he was not as good a figure sculptor. They were followed by the insipid French artist, Esteban de Obray. They worked together with many others in close collaboration but none was particularly outstanding. On the whole they remained untouched by any inspiration from Castile and were mostly influenced from abroad. While they were thus confirming the lack of solidarity between the Levant and Castile there was virtually no artistic activity in Catalonia with the exception of the work of Liatzasolo, whose style is Italianate.

We must now go back to the second decade of the sixteenth century which was of such crucial importance in modern history.

The Catholic king and Cardinal Cisneros were both dead and the future emperor Charles V was still young and full of illusions. He regarded himself as a European and was content to be guided in artistic matters by his chief accountant for Castile, Antonio de Fonseca. The Fonseca family took the place that had formerly been occupied at the court by the Mendozas and were well qualified to give a more classical bias to the Renaissance in Spain; it was with this end in view that they turned to Domenico Fancelli and commissioned him to make two more tombs, but his untimely death occurred in 1518.

Then something happened that was to have a decisive effect on the course of Spanish sculpture. Four Spanish sculptors, Ordóñez, Berruguete, Siloe and Machuca, the "Spanish Eagles" (*Aguilas*) as they were called by Francisco de Holanda, arrived back in Spain. Thenceforth Italy was no longer to be the main source of inspiration for Renaissance art in Spain for all four artists were to effect a Renaissance that was entirely Spanish and wholly un-Italian in spirit. So decisive was the impulse they gave to Spanish art that when foreigners such as Jacopo l'Indaco and Torrigiani came to Spain they were either hispanicized or else completely assimilated – a process that continued until Philip II betrayed the Spanish tradition in his building of the Escorial.

First of the Eagles to make his appearance was Bartolomé Ordóñez, a noble landowner from Burgos. He seems to have been acquainted with Michelangelo's art in Rome, judging by what is supposed to be his first work, the *trasaltar* in Valencia Cathedral with its great alabaster relief of the *Resurrection*. His documented existence began in 1517 when he was commissioned to carve the end panels for the choir-stalls and the sumptuous marble *trascoro* in Barcelona Cathedral. In 1519 the solemn chapter of the Order of the Golden Fleece met under its Grand Master, Charles V, at Barcelona. The king then followed Antonio de Fonseca's sound advice by allowing him to call in Ordóñez to finish the two tombs left unfinished on Fancelli's death, one being destined for Charles's parents, Philip and Joan, and the other for Cardinal Cisneros. Once he had obtained this commission Ordóñez spent the rest of his life in a whirl of activity. He worked so fast that in little more than three years he had practically fulfilled his contracts and had gone to Naples with his fellow Eagle and countryman, Diego Siloe, to decorate a chapel with marble ornaments and an altar.

Ordóñez was the only Spanish sculptor who could vie with Michelangelo among his Italian colleagues and yet keep his own style intact. Whereas Michelangelo created perfect physical forms in every conceivable attitude, only rarely did he express the life of the inner spirit. In contrast, Ordóñez endowed his works with an expressive and delicate sensibility. His great relief of the *Epiphany* for the Caraccioli Chapel at Naples is one of his most perfect works. His medallions for the royal tomb and the panels in the choir-stalls at Barcelona Cathedral are perhaps the finest of their kind, and his ornamentation was equally beautiful, fresh and original in its execution. He founded a school in Naples, but was hardly known in Spain: his royal tomb was hidden away in storage for almost a century (it was only erected in 1603) and he was stifled by the artistic apathy that reigned in Barcelona. He was still young when he died at Carrara in Italy in December 1520.

After Ordóñez had disappeared like a meteor, Spanish sculpture progressed with uncertain step with Siloe alone qualifying as a worthy successor after a period of artistic instability. The third Eagle, Alonso Berruguete, had followed the first two closely after his return from Italy and then appeared at Barcelona as a courtier with the rank of Royal Painter. In 1518 he was at Saragossa where he obtained a contract for the tomb of Charles V's intimate friend, the Chancellor Jean Selvagio or Sauvage, who had just died. Evidence has shown that he was not prepared to carry out such a commission, which required great experience in alabaster carving.

III

In fact, it was only a matter of days before he signed a partnership contract for four years with Felipe Vigarny who probably carved the now existing fragments of the tomb in the museum at Saragossa.

Berruguete next went to Granada to take advantage of the artistic revolution that was being effected in the Royal Chapel where the Catholic monarchs were buried. After a magnificent iron railing had been designed for the chapel, Antonio de Fonseca commissioned Berruguete for a series of frescoes around the altar depicting scenes from the Passion, and other paintings of biblical themes for the sacristy. To Felipe Vigarny went the contract for the altar itself and in 1521 both artists started work in the chapel.

The paintings were never done because of shortage of funds, but the altar was completed. It has long been attributed to Vigarny and it is his greatest work, remaining unsurpassed for its sheer magnificence and powerful emotion. The insipidity and plastic poverty of Castilian figure sculpture had become a thing of the past: Vigarny carved groups of life-size figures with a realism that is almost repellent at times, as in his headless *St John the Baptist* standing between the ferocious executioner and a decorative Salome. But the whole work was carried out in a spirit of restrained classicism with hints of Fancelli's style in the *St George* and the spirited *St James* on horseback, and in scenes from local history representing the capture of Granada and the baptism of the Moors. The reliefs are all set in a framework of Lombard-Renaissance style decorated with shining gilt and a realistic polychromy that was the result of the successful collaboration between Antón de Plasencia and Alonso de Salamanca.

Apart from these reliefs the only other works in the chapel that we can attribute to Vigarny are the praying statues of the Catholic monarchs (now no longer *in situ*), the *Calvary,* the *Pietà* and other less expressive figures. As for the remainder of the work, we know neither the name of the artist nor the source of the initial inspiration. Berruguete naturally springs to mind because of his association with Vigarny, but although his later work was executed with the same *brio*, its technique is quite different. We are therefore left with several unknown factors to take into account while studying the work. As for Berruguete's own commission, the work on two frescoes remained at the stage of preparatory designs, and he spent several years vainly insisting on the validity of his contract. Possibly as a compensation for his neglect, the King made him a scribe in the criminal division of the Valladolid Chancery. To the eventual benefit of art Berruguete's illusions as a court-artist were shattered once and for all.

It is probable that once Berruguete learned of his commission for the paintings he brought two of his supposed collaborators over from Italy in 1520. They were Jacomé Florentín (Jacopo Florentino) and the Toledan Pedro Machuca. As a sculptor Machuca did no more than design the Royal Palace in the Alhambra which, however, was his finest work as an artist. His companion can be identified as Giacomo el Indaco the Elder, a Florentine who was a friend of Michelangelo, whom he had assisted in the paintings for the Sistine Chapel. Both he and Machuca were given an unimportant contract for a side altar in the chapel which was to contain a large triptych by Dieric Bouts, and for various other paintings which they carried out jointly, including the frames and reliefs. Giacomo also drew up designs for the decorations of the chapel and carved a stone *Annunciation,* which is still in existence and deserves attention for its merit and style, on the basis of which several polychrome wood carvings can be attributed to him – especially his finest work, the *Crucifixion* now in Granada.

It would seem to be the result of a sudden burst of inspiration that had lain dormant in Italy and which also needed to express itself in architecture. Giacomo's Plateresque style was even more Spanish in character than that of Machuca's and Siloe's later works. He died in 1525 leaving a follower, Jerónimo Quejano, to carry on his work in Murcia Cathedral. Quejano may also have carved the central portal in the sacristy of Cuenca Cathedral together with a relief of the *Transfiguration* which deserves the very highest praise.

Granada continued to be the imperial capital, thanks to its great monuments and buildings. Many of these had been built with Siloe's assistance after he had left his own province where he had formerly worked with Vigarny in one of the latter's frequent partnerships. Diego Siloe, or Siloee as he signed himself (he was also known as Silohe), was born in Burgos, the son of the great Flemish master Gil, the genius of the monastery at Miraflores. As mentioned above, Siloe first appeared at Naples where he collaborated with Ordóñez in the carving for the altar in the Chapel of S. Giovanni a Carbonara. On his return to Burgos he spent two years sculpting the alabaster tomb of Bishop Acuna and the magnificent *Escalera Dorada* for the cathedral. He may previously have completed the figure sculpture, for the altar of Santa Ana in the Chapel of the Constable which had been left unfinished by his father, where he also collaborated with Vigarny who had returned from Granada. They first worked together on the side altar dedicated to St Peter, which has an additional figure of *St Jerome* recently acknowledged as an outstanding early work by Siloe and, on the basis of its style, proof that he had collaborated with Vigarny on the high altar in the Chapel in 1523.

Although Siloe was working in the Chapel of the Constable in a subordinate capacity to his supposed master, he outclassed Vigarny with the richness of his figure carving, particularly in his female figures with their air of expectant motherhood. He also expressed the spirit of asceticism in his *St Jerome* and the relief of *St John the Baptist* (now in the museum at Valladolid), which seemed to foreshadow his marble *St Sebastian* at Barbadillo with its air of suffering – the finest Spanish work to have been inspired by Michelangelo. Then, although he had no lack of work, Siloe left Burgos and took to the open road, perhaps because he had tired of his surroundings and was suffering from Vigarny's jealousies and rivalry. In 1528 he was called to Granada to take charge of the building of the cathedral, which was just rising from its foundations, and to continue the building of the church of San Jerónimo which had been begun by Giacomo el Indaco. He proved himself the greatest Spanish architect of the century, a masterly designer, expert stone-carver, and a highly original ornamental sculptor. Surrounded by pupils, renowned as a patron and a true Christian gentleman, he stood out as one of the greatest representatives of the Spanish Renaissance and one of its most refined figure sculptors.

We must now return to Berruguete, whom we left at Valladolid where he was working as a scribe, completely cut off from the emperor and his court. For a while he confined his artistic activity to painting but his works were so clumsily executed that they were worthless. In 1527 he finally obtained a contract for the altar in the monastery at La Mejorada after unsuccessful attempts for the commission of gilding and painting of the altar in Oviedo Cathedral. In his work at La Mejorada we would expect to find Berruguete repeating the splendid style he had shown in the Royal Chapel at Granada but we are to be disappointed. The altar recalls the one designed at Granada by Giacomo el Indaco and Machuca and is

14

only sparsely decorated. The figures already have the expressiveness and sense of movement that typify Berruguete's later work, but they are set in a framework that is both faulty and archaic. Far from being Italian in style it resembles the work of another sculptor who was then working in Castile, Juan de Valmaseda, one of Vigarny's pupils and a collaborator in the altar at Oviedo Cathedral. His chief merit resides in the fact that he overcomes his limitations by means of an impassioned sense of movement which heralded the kind of medieval mannerism cultivated by Siloe and Berruguete. His style may be studied in his carvings for the portals in the Hospital del Rey at Burgos, his *Calvary* in Palencia Cathedral and a side altar in León Cathedral, the last being perhaps his best work. He was active between 1514 and 1548.

Once Berruguete had become a mature and experienced sculptor he revealed himself as the interpreter of the Castilian spirit with a profound but bold emotionalism, and a certain unevenness in quality due to his anxiety to excel. After he had discharged his duties at the Valladolid Chancery his art became openly anti-classical. The dramatic qualities of his work do not come from the subject matter itself but from his own passionate inner impulses. He expressed himself with a sense of furious movement in his figures that was to be copied by his followers and regarded as a manifestation of inner spiritual intensity. Towards the end of his career, from 1533 onwards, he surrounded himself with craftsmen of greater technical expertise than himself, as is evident in the choir-stalls in Toledo Cathedral. It is here that Berruguete revolutionized Castilian sculpture while working with Siloe and Vigarny. Siloe had planned the general design for the stalls and Vigarny had made the models and laid down the conditions under which the work was to be executed.

As a disagreement arose between Vigarny and Berruguete, it was decided to share the carving of the stalls between them. Berruguete was regarded as an intruder in Toledo and in order to defend his reputation had to relinquish the carving of the foreground details in his reliefs to his most distinguished followers, Isidro de Villoldo and Francisco Giralte. He then scored a resounding victory over his rival, after Vigarny had died, with a gigantic sculpture of the *Transfiguration* over the choir-stalls. He was less successful with the tomb he was commissioned to sculpt for Cardinal Tavera in 1551. Carving in marble proved to be beyond his technical capacity and he had to call in an expert in this medium: Bautista Vázquez, who was the only classicist in the midst of the host of Toledan figure sculptors. Nevertheless, Vázquez's *Pietà* in Ávila Cathedral and the tomb for the inquisitor Corro in the church of San Vincente de la Barquera at Ávila show him to have been an outstanding artist and one who, like Berruguete, had been able to make a successful transition in his art to the new style.

In the meantime Vigarny had kept up his workshop in Burgos. Evidence that he would occasionally cease work on a commissioned piece may be seen by a comparison of his tomb for Canon Lerma in Burgos Cathedral with the small altar of the *Deposition* in Toledo Cathedral. Both works were carved in alabaster, but whereas the first is well balanced and decorated with elegantly handled medallions, the figures in the second suffer from being too agitated. The composition and design of the altar are confused and the effect is pictorial rather than plastic. Then, in his share of the Toledo choir-stalls, his figures are generally insipid and monotonous except for a few female figures which have a certain grace and elegance and are quite different from his usual style. They must certainly have been carved by Vigarny's son, Gregorio Pardo, judging by their stylistic affinities with the beautiful panel in the archbishop's throne which is documented as being Pardo's work. He must also have carved the two wall-tombs, which have now been removed from their original site at Espejo, even though the work was originally given to his father. They are decorated with beautiful medallions each bearing a figure of the Virgin, a special motif which he repeated several times in smaller works.

From then on Spanish sculpture has to be considered in relation with its polychromy which, together with gilt and *estofado,* did so much to enhance the effect of wood carvings. When they were in Burgos both Siloe and Vigarny were assisted by León Picardo, a great painter of images, who was extremely skilled in *graffito* decoration and painted Italianate *grotteschi* in blue, black and white unsurpassed in quality. Berruguete himself was a painter as well as a sculptor. For the flesh parts he used strong naturalistic colours and made lavish use of gold for the draperies before painting over them; sometimes he also worked in *grisaille,* creating lively subjects that are very characteristic of his style. Polychromy for sculpture also gained ground at Valladolid through the work of other painters. They painted naturalistic foliage patterns in different colours over a gold ground which they then partially uncovered by hatching or scratching away the paint, thus giving the polychromy a remarkably luminous and delicate effect. This was the *estofado* technique as practised by Becerra and his school.

Somewhat earlier in about 1533 a sculptor appeared in León who seemed to have affinities with Berruguete's Baroque style but whose work is principally outstanding for its loving treatment of the human form and the exquisite refinement of its modelling. He was Juan de Juní, probably a Frenchman from the Champagne district, who settled in Valladolid and became acquainted with Berruguete, who praised him highly. Although Juní's earlier figures exhibit a tendency towards meaningless gesticulation, his later work is charged with a profundity of expression that is in perfect harmony with the very essence of the Castilian character which he was to interpret in unprecedentedly violent terms. Of his great works the *Immaculate Conception* at Medina de Rioseco is a sublime expression of ecstasy and the *Virgin of the Swords* the quintessence of sorrow; similarly he succeeded in endowing his *Virgin* in the church of San Segundo, Ávila, with a spirit of withdrawal and his reliquary-bust of Saint Anne with all the grief of her old age. His art is always disciplined and assured and its beauty enhanced by vigorous polychrome and fine *estofado.* The sense of movement in his figures is also apparent in the altarpieces with their curving patterns and lively ornamentations inspired by Juní's northern sense of fantasy. His style is not Gothic; rather it constitutes a break with classical ideals. He gave proof of a new and original decorative sense in the design of his altars with their structural perspective and distribution of reliefs according to varying planes of depth. Were it not for the excessive ornateness of his draperies and the total absence of the nude in his work he could be considered a follower of Michelangelo; in any case, he may justifiably be called a precursor of Bernini's Baroque style.

The old Moorish art of stucco decoration was renewed and practised by Juní and, apart from his pupils, by the family of Corral de Villalpando, who used this medium for their architectural decorations throughout the Tierra de Campos. The cheapness and speed of this process produced an abundance of figures and relief ornamentation in polychrome stucco, examples of which are to be found in the Benavente chapel at Medina de Rioseco, created by Jerónimo de Corral in 1546, and in the Casa Blanca at Medina del Campo. Corral's technical

V

mastery was only surpassed by his fertile creative sense. His figure scenes and caprices are masterpieces full of spontaneous inspiration, and form a fitting conclusion to the great eruption of Renaissance Baroque in Castile.

From 1542 onwards the work of another great sculptor appeared in Toledo Cathedral. This was Nicolás de Vergara, a skilled and erudite designer whose art ranked as high as that of Berruguete. Vergara inspired his son, Nicholas the Younger, and another member of the Corral family, Francisco de Villalpando, who were both expert bronze sculptors, as is proved by their lecterns in the choir of Toledo Cathedral and, among other masterpieces, the railings they made for the tomb of Cardinal Cisneros. Another artist who worked in their midst carving altars was Bautista Vázquez who has already been cited for his skill in sculpting marble. He later went to Seville where his style underwent a revolutionary change. On the whole, the work of these artists was marked by its refined classicism, severe discipline and a coolness, all due to Italian influences, and exemplified in the bronze figures which Leone Leoni made for the Emperor in 1556.

At about the same time, the famous painter Gaspar Becerra came to Spain from Rome where he had been inspired by the Mannerist style of Michelangelo's art which was to develop in his pupils in a typically Spanish form. Becerra worked successfully with these stylistic formulae in his retreat from those of nature, and produced several fine works by following already hallowed traditions. He soon became a sculptor and in 1558-62 carved the great altar in Astorga Cathedral which was afterwards widely copied by his pupils. The classical restraint of his art was repeated by his follower Esteban Jordán, whose chief work was the altar of St Mary Magdalene at Valladolid which dates from 1571. A somewhat different path was followed by Juan de Ancheta, who had been previously influenced by Juní, translating the latter's expressive vigour into empty posturing, as in the colossal figures on the altar of the convent at Briviesca, which may have been entirely by his own hand and which started a fashion in Burgos, Pamplona, Saragossa and Jaca. In Navarre the outstanding artists seem to have been Andrés de Araoz, who carved the altars at Genevilla and Lapoblación, and the monk Juan de Beauvais, who created equally fine altars at Estella and Unzu. Taken as a whole their work is proof of a stable and coherent artistic impulse which, by its elegance, has affinities with the sculpture in Santo Domingo de la Calzada. Although many foreigners came to work in the region, they wrought no stylistic changes; rather they seem to have passively embraced the idiom of the local school.

By way of contrast, the Mannerist style spread throughout New Castile after the initial impetus was given by Pompeo Leoni who had come to Spain to work for Philip II in 1556, to complete the bronze figures begun by his father, Leone. He came under the influence of the Castilian environment and eventually carved altars in the Spanish manner, which were masterly adaptations of an Italianism that was at the same time more classical than Becerra's and more virile than that of Vázquez. Being a good portraitist, his work was full of naturalism and he showed his sense of the grandiose in the royal tombs he carved for the Escorial, of such a size as to fill the whole chapel with emotion. He started the fashion for kneeling tomb effigies which are so frequently found in Castile and he gave his Crucifixions an air of overpowering majesty. An artist who blossomed in Leoni's orbit was Juan Bautista de Monegro who may have been the sculptor chosen by El Greco to carve the gilt figures in the round to decorate his altar for Santo Domingo el Antiguo at Toledo. They are outstandingly elegant works and, with their long simple flow of draperies, quite different from the usual style as practised at Toledo. An artist who developed outside Leoni's group was Domingo Beltrán from Ávila. This sculptor had joined the Jesuits in 1561 as a lay brother and had then gone to study art in Rome. His stay in Italy accounts for the difference and progress shown in his art, from the time he made the figures for the church of Santiago at Medina del Campo, to the altar he carved in Murcia after his return from Rome. The earlier works are carried out in a pedestrian manner, but the later figures are classical in style, finely proportioned and full of emotion. The culminating work of his career is the admirable *Christ of the Doctrines* at Alcalá de Henares, which he sculpted after he had come into contact with the artists working in the Escorial. It is his last work, probably completed in 1591, the year of his death.

Castilian sculpture continued to be practised in a disciplined, mannered spirit inspired by what were regarded as classical models, by such artists as Giraldo de Merlo in Toledo, Pedro de la Cuadro and Francisco de Rincón at Valladolid, among others who became increasingly decadent, until finally Gregorio Fernández gave the *coup de grâce* to the whole school. By then Philip II was already dead, and with him vanished Spanish supremacy and the spirit of the Renaissance.

To see how the transition was made from the old to the new style we have to turn to the two great centres of sculpture in Andalusia: Granada and Seville. The city that typified the gaiety of Andalusia and the spirit of adventure inspired by the beckoning ocean was Seville, while Granada withdrew into seclusion beneath the peaks of the Sierra Nevada and under the towers of the Alhambra, which bore silent witness to the triumph of Castile over Islam. It was here that the Catholic kings wanted to be buried, next to the cathedral which had echoed with the hymns of the triumphant Christians. The emperor's wish to lie with his ancestors was not to be granted, nor was he able to enjoy his palace in the Alhambra which was begun under his orders in 1526. The designs for the palace were drawn up by the painter Pedro Machuca who had become an architect. Although he followed the refinements of the Roman style as practised in Italy, he impressed his absolute originality on the whole structure. Despite the fact that he had not practised sculpture himself, he made his colleague Esteban Sánchez into an accomplished figure sculptor, and he decorated the palace with allegorical and historical scenes in relief under the guiding hand of his son-in-law, Juan de Orea. Both Machuca and Orea designed the marble figures carved by the Milanese Nicolo de Corte and the Fleming Antonio de Leval. Their combined work is aristocratic, exquisite and almost perfect in its execution, but it lacks life and has no real roots. Meanwhile Siloe was working in Granada Cathedral, whence his genius shone over half of Spain, producing pupils who assisted him with his innumerable decorations. Diego de Aranda was Siloe's most faithful follower and Baltasar de Arce, the most vigorous, but when the great master died in 1563 there was no one to inherit his genius, until an unknown artist, Diego de Pesquera, suddenly made his appearance. He may have come from Burgos and it seems fairly certain he had studied at Rome as one of Michelangelo's followers. An attractive artistic personality is revealed in his altar and especially in the cathedral where he worked mainly on the tower and on a nearby portal. The delicacy of his modelling is that of a virtuoso and he was able to bring an emotion to his figures which, although less moving, had affinities with Siloe's work. He later went to Seville and in 1580 he disappeared.

At that time Seville was the great market for the wealth of the Indies. It overflowed with luxury, the inhabitants devoted themselves to pleasure and had little inclination for hard work. Although the city produced no schools of art, it was embellished with magnificent imported works and gave shelter to a select number of artists, including Pietro Torrigiani, the most famous and also the most frustrated of the many who worked in Seville. He had been Michelangelo's rival and came from England in about 1525, attracted to Spain by the lustre of her imperial grandeur. The only commissions he could obtain were for sculptures in the poorest of all materials: painted terracotta, which was a traditional Sevillean art. Among the artists who had worked in this medium were Lorenzo Mercadante, the greatest of all terracotta sculptors in Spain, the Fleming Pedro Millán at the end of the fifteenth century, who had made some beautiful figures, and Jorge Fernández, probably a German, whose finest work had been his carving for the cathedral altar, but who also produced terracotta figures to decorate the *ciborium* in 1509, and finally the Frenchman, Miguel Perrín who worked after 1517. He was a Renaissance artist, his masterpiece being the group of the *Lamentation* made for the Cathedral of Santiago de Compostela. Torrigiani's finest terracotta figures are a *Virgin and Child* and a penitent *St Jerome*. Both works are perfectly modelled and anatomically correct but they lack depth of feeling, for the artist was too self-centred to absorb the essential Spanish ideals.

Many foreign artists continued to come to Andalusia. Guillén Ferrant and Roque de Bolduque collaborated on the altar of Santa Maria at Cáceres but there is more affectation than any real feeling in their work. Their basically stylized images underlie the Spanish elements that were added only later. The Spanish style is represented by a follower of Berruguete, Isidro de Villoldo and, to much better effect, by Bautista Vázquez who was the real patriarch of the school of Seville with his classically inspired figures. He was also outstanding among his contemporaries for his carving of marble. Similarly Pesquera distinguished himself with his bronze figures, practising the art in Seville where he may have been the apprentice to an Italian artist. Both Vázquez and Pesquera worked in stone and decorated the ante-room and Capitulary Hall of the cathedral with the assistance of Diego de Velasco and Jerónimo Hernández, who created very elegant and surprisingly modern-looking figures and set the pattern for all future representations of the penitent St Jerome. They were followed by Andrés de Ocampo who exaggerated the flow of draperies in his figures, and Gaspar Nuñez Delgado, who was both a talented terracotta sculptor and ivory worker. They both continued to work into the seventeenth century. Juan Bautista Vázquez, 'El Mozo' (the Younger) has been credited with the great altar at San Jerónimo at Granada, where a school of figure sculptors was formed with Pablo de Rojas at its head. The latter specialized in Crucifixions inspired by Leoni's work, and he left a pupil, Juan Martínez Montañés, who was to achieve the transition in seventeenth-century Andalusian art from Mannerism to Baroque, but without, however, any sign of a definite break between the two styles.

So far we have seen how the sixteenth century in Spain was inspired by the Italian Renaissance, accepting its forms while rejecting its pagan elements, and reviving the medieval Christian spirit that became the very essence of the new art. We have seen that Ordóñez, Siloe and Jacopo Florentino were the foremost exponents of the classical style in Spain, while behind them came Zarza, Vigarny and Joly, who were less Italianate in their art, making up a great school of disciplined academicians. We have also seen that Berruguete evolved a style of expression which was quite opposed to classicism, and that Vergara and Becerra responded by adopting a disciplined Mannerism inspired by the art of the Leonis, while Juní, Vázquez and Pesquera revived the element of emotionalism. But what we have not seen is the emergence of a homogeneous style in Spanish sculpture, or a national school like those formed in Italy and even in France by Michelangelo and Bernini. As a result Spanish sculpture appears disorientated to the critical eye. The truth is that it did not depend on either the classical tradition or its antithesis, but found its true source in the inherited medieval spirit with all its honesty, its religious feeling, its individuality, and its polychromy, all almost exclusively devoted to pious ends. Its imagery remained traditional with the figures of the Virgin and Christ on the Cross presiding over scenes from the Bible and lives of the great saints, as well as of local saints. Sepulchres became adjuncts of altars, and apart from the palace at Granada and the royal effigies there was very little profane art of any worth.

Spanish art of the eighteenth century developed its own resources. Italy had become a foreign country again, and Bernini's academic Baroque was regarded unsympathetically, for inspiration was henceforth to come from reality alone. The glories of the sixteenth century, when Spain had been an illustrious economic power, began to appear as little more than a courtly fiction. As Spain's vital centres declined and the country had to face the consequences of inevitable bad government, there was a return to reality and the people turned again toward Heaven in a revival of piety. As the people of Spain took the lead in this kind of spiritual reappraisal it became reflected in the art of the time. Churches were taken over by confraternities and charitable institutions which renewed religious art in accordance with their own taste. There was to be less profane art than ever before; there were no more tomb sculptures and instead processional figures predominated in sculpture.

At the beginning of the seventeenth century there was a new king and a new court at Valladolid and it was here that sculpture was revitalized by Gregorio Fernández. He was commissioned by Philip III to make a Dead Christ for the royal oratory and the result was the famous *Pardo Christ* shown lying on an altar-cloth with cushions under the head. It is a completely realistic work and had an enormous success. It was copied many times and regarded in Castile as the icon *par excellence*. Nothing that Fernández later created could rival it in its perfection.

Fernández first appeared in Valladolid as a pupil of Francisco de Rincón, who belonged to the school of Pompeo Leoni. After 1606 Fernández showed himself to be completely indifferent to any sort of formula. He broke away from the Mannerist convention with its typical treatment of costume in which the draperies swirl obliquely round the body in carefully balanced curves and in which all the masses are systematically composed. Instead he used draperies as a single piece and, rather than allowing them to reveal the volume of his figures, he let them fall down the body in arbitrarily chosen lines and planes. Each figure was conceived separately from the others. Although the gestures contribute to the expressiveness, faces are the focus of attention. There, spiritual depth is allied to a relentless surface realism which can

VII

20

even become repellent, as in certain figures of torturers and hangmen. Renaissance dignity had become a thing of the past and coarseness and ugliness were no longer qualities to be excluded from sculpture. Fernández's statues are always alive and always human. Although their carving is generally disciplined they also suffer from carelessness, lack of balance, and lapses into sheer bad taste due to excessive haste on the artist's part. We have to distinguish between Fernández's own work and the products of his workshop, which necessarily increased with time. Among the latter are the figures made to be carried in procession during Holy Week. These statues show the intrusion of the then prevalent coarseness. Some of Fernández's own compositions, such as the *Vision of St Simon Stock,* show a deplorable lack of unity and expression in contrast to his fine *Baptism of Christ* and his magnificent *Assumption* for the altar in Plasencia Cathedral. With regard to his single figures it is perhaps unfortunate that his statue of the penitent *Magdalene* was regarded as the ideal type to represent female asceticism. Although his statues of Jesuit saints are conventional in their representation, they are full of life, and the expressions of his Dolorosas have a serenity which is devoid of exaggerated pathos.

Fernández had been worried about his precarious health since 1620, and he died in 1636 at the age of sixty. His style had so rapidly become widespread that the figures in the altar of the *Incarnation* in Madrid were attributed to him until it was discovered that they had been carved by a certain Juan González in 1616. The great altar at Peñaranda (carved in 1618 by two obscure artists, Sebastian Ducete and Esteban de Rueda, natives of Toro) closely resembles the master's style and would not be unworthy of his hand. The school which he founded lasted so long that when the figures in the doors of the new cathedral at Salamanca had to be completed the work was done by one of his most faithful followers, Juan Rodríguez, who came all the way from Valladolid, where another of his pupils, Antonio de Paz, had also been working since 1628. The figures in the sacristy of the church of San Esteban and the beautiful *Assumption* were carved by De Paz who may also have been the creator of the exquisite *Immaculate Conception* in the same chapel, which is inspired by Fernández's figures. Francisco de Moure was another pupil who became famous in Galicia for his altar for the Jesuits at Monforte, which was a frankly Baroque piece of work. He worked on it from 1613 to 1636, the year of his death. In Barcelona both Agustín Pujol and his son of the same name became famous; their work was more disciplined and finely modelled than that of the Galician. A more mysterious work, whose creator remains unidentified, is the statue of *St John the Baptist* in Astorga Cathedral, a strikingly pathetic work dating from 1660.

Madrid in the meantime had remained faithful to Pompeo Leoni's classicism, which was maintained by his pupils Alonso de Vallejo and Antón de Moreles. It was only in 1624 that a sculptor of any real originality made his appearance, in the person of Manuel Pereyra, a Portuguese, who sculpted figures for the portals of Madrid churches and of the Jesuit church at Alcalá de Henares. They are so simply and naturally carved that they have received less attention than his stone sculpture of *Saint Bruno,* now in the Academia of San Fernando, which is an outstandingly powerful and original work. In contrast, his other statue of the same saint in the Carthusian monastery at Miraflores is wholly realistic and admirably expressive. But his most unusual work was his statue of *Christ the Intercessor* kneeling on the globe, which is still in its original site at Comillas; his most graceful work, the *Crucifixion,* is in

VIII

21

Segovia Cathedral. In its general features Pereyra's art was so alien to the traditional Castilian style that he may well have been influenced by Alonso Cano who had been living in Madrid since 1638, and who in turn may equally well have inspired Juan Sánchez Barba in his beautiful *Crucifixion* and *Immaculate Conception*. A later pupil of Cano's was Sebastián de Herrera Barnuevo, whose workshop was frequented by José de Mora about 1667. The Granadine Mora was appointed Royal Sculptor and revolutionized figure sculpture in Madrid, giving it an unprecedented intensity of emotion. This trend had already been begun in 1663 by another famous Granadine, Pedro de Mena, who helped to raise sculpture to the same heights then being attained by the court painters.

Meanwhile Andalusia was overflowing with artistic activity. Sebastián and Francisco de Solís carved the figures for the Santo Rastro altar in Jaén Cathedral at the beginning of the century, and after 1617 the lay cleric Juan de Solís, who worked largely for the inquisitor Pacheco, represented a new classicist movement with his statues of the *Immaculate Conception*. At Granada Bernabé de Gaviria worked along the same lines as Gregorio Fernández, but with greater freedom. He had worked in partnership with Pablo de Rojas in 1603 but later left the employment of his patrons, who were unsympathetic to the classical style. In 1614 he carved his colossal group of the Apostles for the *capilla mayor* in Granada Cathedral. He represented all his figures as sinners in a state of exaltation, each holding up the instruments by which he was put to death. With its agitated draperies, dented with deep folds and furrows, each statue has an individual sense of movement and seems almost about to speak. In no similar series of statues has the treatment of each figure been so original and so eloquent.

After Gaviria's death in 1622 the next independent Granadine sculptor of any note was Alonso de Mena.

He had been apprenticed to Andrés de Ocampo at Seville when he was only fifteen and his style principally consists of a relentless realism which was never surpassed. Examples of his work are his statue of *Santiago Matamoros* in the cathedral, where the saint is represented as a contemporary nobleman in full armour with a wide brimmed hat, his sword held high; his *Saint Roch* dressed as a pilgrim of St James with all his travelling equipment, and his *Virgin of Bethlehem* as a finely-dressed lady seated on a chair gazing at the Child lying carelessly on her lap. Both the statues of the *Virgin* and the *Immaculate Conception* are dressed in the fashion of the time, double tunics with wide trailing sleeves, girdles and necklaces of pearls and precious fabrics, and their drapery is generally enhanced by the rich polychromy of elegant floral patterns painted over a gold ground. The statue of *St Michael* is that of a handsome young man in Roman soldier's uniform, with a forelock coming down on his forehead as worn by the youths of Mena's time. All his statues have the same impassive, detached expression.

Mena's most influential work was his famous *Crucifixion* for the church of San José in Madrid. It is carved in unpainted wood and the dying Christ is represented with His feet apart, crucified with four instead of the customary three nails. Other powerful works include his *Christ Kneeling* holding His tunic which was formerly at Alcalá la Real, and his *Ecce Homo* in the church of San Antón, Granada. Despite their plastic shortcomings, all these works show Mena to have been one of the great revolutionary sculptors of his time. He died in 1646 leaving an eighteen-year-old son, Pedro, to carry on his work and to become Alonso Cano's favourite pupil, and an important artist in his own right.

IX

22

The great renovator of Sevillian sculpture was Juan Martínez Montañés who had trained at Granada under Pablo de Rojas whose own style was an imitation of Vázquez's Mannerism. Accordingly, when Montañés moved to Seville in 1587, before he was twenty, he found himself at home among friendly and equally talented colleagues. The most outstanding among them were Andrés de Ocampo and Gaspar Núñez Delgado, who had both been pupils of Jerónimo Hernández. Although Ocampo was exceptionally gifted he remained content to copy his master instead of trying to excel him, but Delgado was more independent and proved himself an innovator with the first representation of the *Immaculate Conception* in the parish church of San Andrés and his *St John the Baptist* for the monastery of San Clemente, both statues of singular power and personality. Delgado also made clay models of the *Ecce Homo* showing great feeling and a profound knowledge of anatomy. These models were afterwards painted by Francisco Pacheco. Between 1585 and 1599 Delgado carved marble *Crucifixions* showing the Dying Christ instead of the Dead Christ, which was an iconographic innovation. Although the Crucifixions were of uneven quality, they received such acclaim that Montañés took them as models for his own works, which earned him the praise of Velázquez who declared that he was a pupil of Becerra's.

Martínez Montañés may have begun working under Becerra's influence which would account for the impulsive tone of his first known work, the *San Cristobal* of 1597, and his expressive and realistic *St Jerome* of Llerena which takes after Becerra's style rather than that of Torrigiani. He then revealed his own personality in his famous *Christ of Clemency*, completed in 1606, for the sacristy in Seville Cathedral. From that time onwards his art was to be nourished by a fervent piety which gave his works a serene, peaceful quality although their attitudes and the treatment of their costumes followed the Mannerist sytle of Vázquez. His statues are distinguished by their naturalism and deep inner feeling, as in his penitent *St Dominic* with its restrained anatomical treatment in strong contrast to that of *St Jerome,* its naturalism reinforced by Pacheco's painting of the flesh parts. The same qualities are present in Montañés's heads of Jesuit saints and his *Christ of the Passion* with its majestic air of resignation. He gradually paid less attention to the carving of the limbs of his figures, covering them with pieces of canvas that had been dipped in glue and then painted, or with rich pieces of cloth, as feminine prudery began to make its influence felt in the arts.

The *Immaculate Conception* was one of Montañés's favourite themes, repeated many times from his first version for the church of San Pedro, with its singular sweetness of expression, to his statue for the cathedral in 1630 which has an air of radiant intimacy that may have been derived from Cano, who was then making his influence felt. His other figures and his reliefs with their background of landscape, carefully composed after Delgado's style, are full of the same serenity and a kind of classical, even archaic simplicity. His figures of St John the Baptist are outstandingly original, particularly the kneeling statue for the convent of San Leandro and his final representation of the saint for the church of Santa Paula in 1638. His last work was the *Battle of the Angels* for San Miguel in Jerez de la Frontera, with its audacious representation of devils in human form. Its impact is as disturbing as that of many of his earlier works.

It is hard to consider Montañés's most faithful follower, Juan de Mesa, in isolation from his master. In his twelve years of activity, from 1615 until 1627, he produced a great number

x

23

of Crucifixions in the same style. The most notable for their agonized expressions and the amount of devotion they inspired are his *Dead Christ of Love* with its impressive countenance, his *Christ of Vergara,* and his *Jesus del Gran Poder* for the church of San Lorenzo. Their style is so close to that of Montañés that they were all attributed to him until proved otherwise by documentation.

The progress of Sevillian sculpture in the seventeenth century in harmony with the spirit of the times is in no small measure due to Alonso Cano. He was born into the profession and spent the first fifteen years of his life among sculptors but in 1616 he moved to Seville to study painting under Francisco Pacheco. He was obsessed with the idea of making a name as a painter, as he regarded painting as the most progressive and socially important of the arts. After practising for some time, a crisis of discouragement made him return to sculpture. From 1629 he assisted his father in his profession of carving altars but after ten years another crisis in his life made him down his tools and go to Madrid. There he was patronised by Count Olivares who appointed him as his official painter.

To gauge Cano's success as a sculptor one has only to enumerate his works. Each one started a new trend in Christian iconography. His figures are marked by an inner spirit, constantly pensive expressions, life-like gestures and anatomical structure, and an unfailing individuality, even when they are copies of foreign works. Their technical perfection extends to their naturalistic polychromy which Cano had learned from Pacheco. Cano was a friend and follower of Montañés, rather than his pupil. We have to accept the attribution of his early works on trust, as documentary evidence is lacking. His statue of *St Teresa* echoes the style of Gaviria who may have been his first master at Granada; and his second *Immaculate Conception* in the church of San Andrés is a copy of Montañés's work in San Pedro, although its expression is quite different, while his other representation of the same theme in the church of San Julián only differs from Montañés's style by its more delicate modelling. Then in 1629 he was commissioned to sculpt a *Virgin and Child* for the high altar of Santa Maríá at Lebrija. Cano himself took pride in this work which shows a complete break with Montañés's style. It is a majestic figure with its steady gaze, its flowing mantle gathered in around its feet, and its Child, naked in the classical tradition. It represents the beginning of Cano's own personal conception of beauty. He created another masterpiece with his youthful *St John the Baptist,* now in the Güell Collection in Barcelona, which inspired Montañés's similar figure in the Convent of Santa Ana. Cano invested this work with a modern realism which can be regarded as almost vulgar.

Once Cano was in Madrid he returned to painting for a while but without any great success. However, his drawings show the masterly vigour with which he attacked his subjects. It was he, rather than the inaccessible Velázquez, who headed the school of Madrid and instead of making sculptures he painted canvases of single figures for the altars at Getafe. He only sculpted for a few special commissions, producing some small figures such as a *St Anthony carrying the Infant Christ,* an iconographical innovation, a dead *St Francis,* which had a vast success and was greatly copied, and an enchanting *Infant Jesus* with wonderfully detailed polychromy.

In 1652 Cano returned to Granada to seek the tranquillity that was always eluding him and to appease his troubled soul by taking up ecclesiastical duties. He found the environment stimulating and his output increased. The first sculpture of his last period was his *Immaculate*

Conception, for the sacristy of the cathedral, which had great depth of feeling, its elegant silhouette receding towards its slender base. Cano had begun carving figures of this type with his *Virgin* at Lebrija and repeated the pattern in other statues of his final period, including his seated *Virgin of Bethlehem* in the Cathedral. His activity expanded in his last years and included the planning of architectural projects, designing and decorating the Church of the Guardian Angel, for which he made a marble statue of the titular saint besides statues of *St Anthony* and *St Diego.* Besides these magnificent statues with their lively polychromy, Cano collaborated on two other companion-pieces with his pupil Pedro de Mena. In a final burst of creativity Cano carved the huge busts of *St Paul* and *Adam* and *Eve* which would have been worthy of the Renaissance artists of Florence. They were not conceived as portraits, for their marvellously realistic and majestic countenances were entirely inspired by Cano's wonderful imagination. He died in 1667.

Alonso de Mena's son, Pedro, worked in the same realistic style as Cano and proved himself to be a fine craftsman. He imitated Cano's work closely, as can best be seen in his first sculpture, an *Immaculate Conception* in the parish church at Alhendín, and assisted the master in the carving of his *Immaculate Conception* for Granada Cathedral. After his own and Cano's statues had been completed in 1656 they collaborated on the four figures for the Convent of the Angel, Mena carving the *St Joseph* and the *St Peter of Alcantará.* The following year Cano had asked for the contract to carve the figures for the choir in Málaga Cathedral but because of the jealousies that he aroused he handed over the commission to Mena who left Granada in 1658, settling in Málaga until his death thirty years later.

Mena's wood carving is masterly, and he was able to impart the appearance of life to the surfaces of his statues. His figures in the choir at Málaga Cathedral are beautiful and original, which is more than can be said for most of his work, confined as is usually was to a rather vulgar realism and to imitations. His statue of the *Magdalene,* now in the Museum at Valladolid, is one of his best works. In its warmth of feeling and humanity it surpasses the similar statue by Gregorio Fernández which Mena took as his model. His *St Francis* in Toledo Cathedral was another famous work but copied from Cano, as was his *Immaculate Conception* in the sacristy, a subject which he repeated many times in slightly differing versions. His carving is always graceful and restrained but is apt to lack vigour and character. As he grew older his art degenerated and he handed over his work to pupils who produced a great number of statues, mostly of monks. The effigies of the Catholic kings at prayer in Granada Cathedral were the only secular figures to come from his workshop. Because of his lack of strong personality his later works tended towards the Baroque, but his earlier figures were distinguished by their remarkable simplicity, as for example *St Benedict* and *St Bernard* in the monasteries of their orders at Granada. They may have served as models for his later works, and in themselves they are not without merit.

While Mena was working in his quietist style, another family of sculptors achieved prominence in Granada. The first to appear was Bernardo de Mora, a native of Majorca who had settled in Granada in 1650 and worked in Cano's workshop, replacing Mena after he had gone to Malaga. He carved a beautiful but somewhat feminine statue of St Michael for the hermitage of that saint, and specialised in *imagenes de vestir,* in which only the feet and head are carved, the rest being covered by real costumes, reserving his talent for the expression in their features. His statue of *San Juan de Dios* emphasized his dependence on Cano's style which he transmitted to his son, José de Mora. In 1665 father and son collaborated in the sculptures for the façade of the sanctuary of the *Virgin of Sorrows*. Later José went to Madrid where he remained, with a few intervals, from 1668 until 1680, becoming Royal Sculptor. He carved, among other works, an *Immaculate Conception* for the church of San Isidro. This was inspired by Cano's similar statue and had cherubs' heads carved around the base in a style he repeated later in Granada. There he made a *Soledad* for the church of Santa Ana, full of the feeling with which he was beginning to endow his images and which was to be taken to extremes in his many statues of the *Ecce Homo* and *Dolorosa* which were widely copied. Practically all his other figures expressed the same kind of highly concentrated anguish in a manner that was both original and realistic, unlike the morbid and anaemic style of other artists. His other notable works are his two contrasting statues of *St Bruno,* his martyred *St Pantaleon,* his elegant *St Pascual,* his *Santa Rosa* of Viterbo which almost seems to speak, and his *Christ of Salvation* in the church of San José, a tremendously powerful and original work in its anatomical structure and impression of death. Mora enhanced the realism of his statues by using pieces of cloth soaked in glue for the draperies, often painting them himself. Sometimes he was so carried away by his artistic passion that he suffered mild fits of insanity. His work constitutes a worthy ending to the school of Andalusia which exerted such influence, with its obsessive but humanized ideals of piety. It was without artifice on the whole and was not only anti-classical but also anti-Baroque, except on the few occasions when chance or a momentary superficial attraction drew it towards those styles.

In the eighteenth century José's younger brother Diego de Mora and his pupil José Risueño were only moderately Baroque in their style. They were followed somewhat later by the last interpreter of Cano's art, Torcuato Ruiz del Peral. On the other hand, Seville succumbed to Bernini's influence, as may be seen in the two Italian statues in the hospital of La Caridad and in the much earlier work of the Fleming José de Haerts, or Arce, who was active after 1636 until his death some thirty years later, and who showed a certain Baroque influence. This influence was first seen in his sculpture of a group of Apostles for the Carthusian monastery at Jerez; accompanied by Montañés in this change of style he finished the altar of *San Miguel* in the same city and finally carved the huge stone images in the sacristy of Seville Cathedral. His rhetorical figures, free rendering of sumptuous draperies, and dignified classic naturalism betray his complete break with Montañés's style. Although his work is neglected at present it was well enough received at the time, and he certainly had an influence on Alonso Cano who vouched for him in his contract with the monastery at Jerez. Another outstanding member of the group was Felipe de Rivas who carved the intriguing altar of *St John the Baptist* in the church of Santa Paula.

The Baroque style was openly championed by Alfonso Martínez who carved the *Great Conception* in Seville Cathedral, and Francisco Antonio Gijón whose *Dead Christ* at Triana was popularly known as *El Cachorro,* but the leading sculptor was Pedro Roldán who had worked under Alonso de Mena at Granada, became acquainted with Montañés in 1646 and who died in 1700. His most spectacular works were his *Burial of Christ* together with its enclosing altarpiece in the Caridad hospital and a similar group for the sanctuary. In the second work his composition is more successful, and he managed to combine Baroque forms

XI

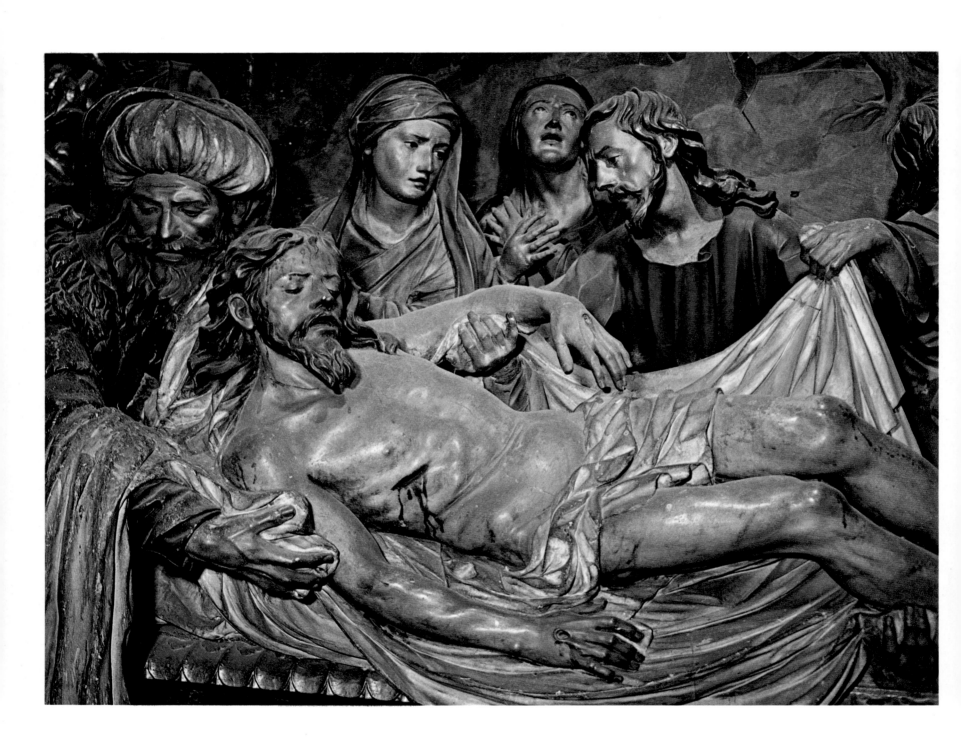

with traditional Spanish naturalism. His *St Ferdinand* dressed in seventeenth-century armour and his *St Peter* in papal costume show his master Mena's influence, just as his statue of *St Joseph* echoes Cano's style. He was followed by his daughter Luisa 'La Roldana' and his grandson Pedro Duque Cornejo, who completely broke with the traditional style and with whom our survey of Spanish sculpture comes to an end.

With the advent of the Bourbons to the Spanish throne the fine arts turned for inspiration to France, where the Baroque had long been established since its arrival from Italy. It was exalted in Spain and even found popular favour, for the exaggeration suited the mood of the time which had produced the Churrigueresque revolution in architectural decoration. The Catalan Luis Bonifas and the Murcian Francisco Salcillo upheld in sculpture the traditional ideals of emotional piety in contrast to the school of Madrid. But whereas Goya was brilliantly to re-assert the Spanish spirit in painting, a talented courtly school of sculpture ensured the survival of foreign styles. Essentially Spanish characteristics survived only in the humble terracotta figures made in Andalusia with their representations of shepherds, bull-fighters and gypsies in a style that was partly popular, partly romantic. It was folk art, an art that knew neither sorrow nor glory in its brief life. The last significant terracotta sculptor was the Granadine Antonio Peñas y León who was active about 1860.

XII

14

16

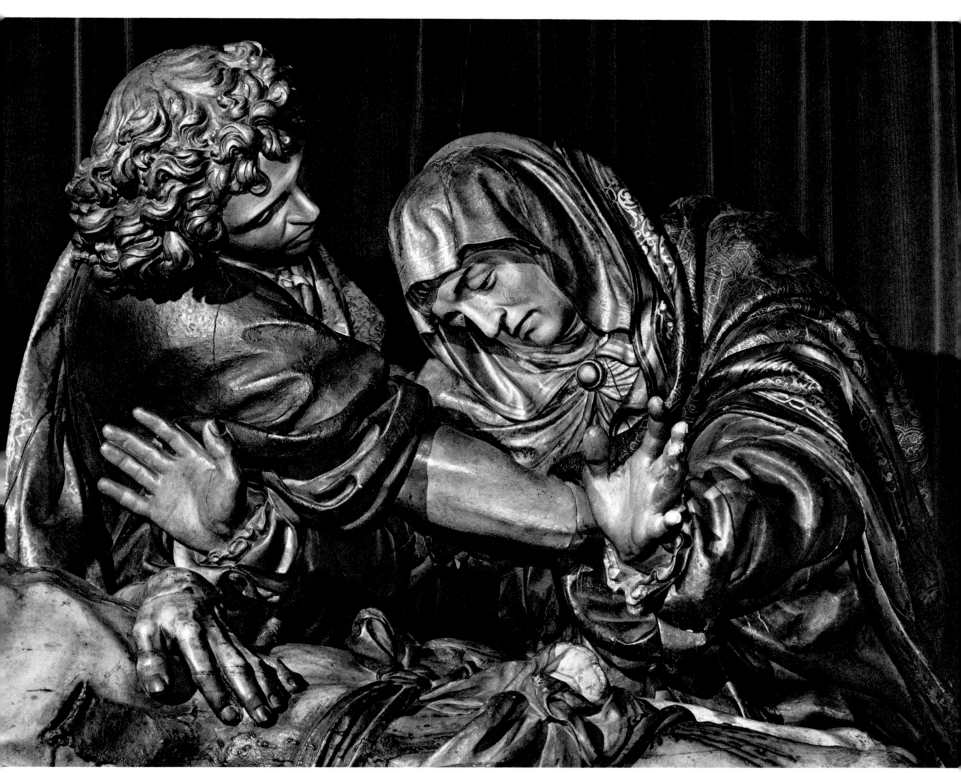

46

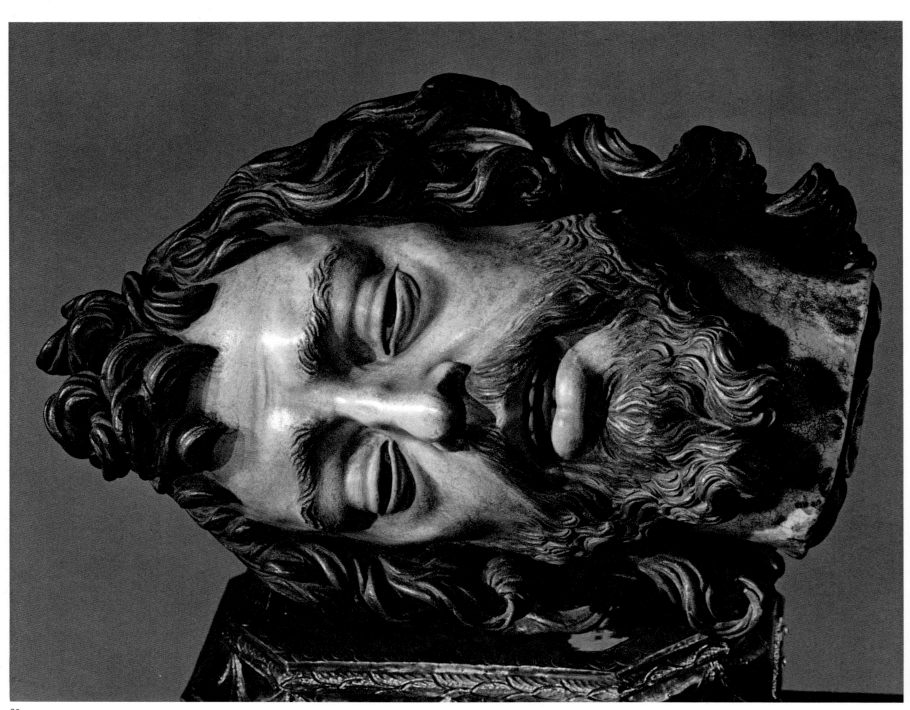

68

70

74

NOTES ON THE COLOUR PLATES

Frontispiece: PEDRO DE MENA: DOLOROSA.
MONASTERY OF LAS DESCALZAS REALES, MADRID.

Mena created a new type of imagery that became widespread in Granadine sculpture with his pairs of busts or half-length figures of the *Ecce Homo* and the *Dolorosa*. Of the many versions made, the finest is that in the monastery of Las Descalzas Reales in Madrid. In its perfection of carving the *Dolorosa* is much finer than the accompanying *Ecce Homo,* but such disparity was characteristic of Mena who could never succeed in giving his Christs the right combination of majesty and suffering for them to achieve their full effect. His Virgins, on the other hand, were always successful in their impression of deeply felt emotion, and the example illustrated surpasses all the others.

As is proved by his signature, Mena made both the *Dolorosa* and her companion piece at Málaga in 1673. The figure is carved in half-length and is wearing a crimson tunic, white veil and a blue mantle. There is a touch of affectation in her attitude, one hand being extended and the other pressed to her bosom, but this is an insignificant fault compared with the marvellous rendering of the head which is modelled with unrivalled delicacy. The slight furrow in her brow, her reddened downcast eyes, her tensed facial muscles, the tears on her cheeks and her half-open mouth are all signs of her grief – a sorrow so deeply felt it goes beyond all tears. Her emotion is mute, expressed without drama or agitation: the youthful beauty of her features is scarcely disfigured by her inconsolable sorrow.

Mena executed this figure with the greatest simplicity. The carving is extremely sober and relies for its effect on delicacy of detail, all due entirely to the chisel, since Mena made no use of secondary materials, such as fabrics stiffened with glue, even for the finest parts of the draperies, which are all carved with simplicity and elegance. Equally artistic is the polychromy which is in perfect harmony with the carving: a light brown for the face, a clear shade of chestnut brown with touches of gilt for the smooth flow of hair, and white for the veil. The Virgin's head is covered with a dark blue mantle falling below her long neck and revealing the crimson tunic underneath.

Mena has indeed moved far away from the violence of Juan de Juní's grief-stricken Virgins! His *Dolorosa* is full of the quietist inward sorrow of the Andalusians which disdains outward show and prefers to hide itself in solitude.

I. FELIPE VIGARNY DE BORGOÑA: SAINT MATTHEW: RELIEF FROM THE ALTARPIECE OF THE ROYAL CHAPEL, GRANADA (DETAIL).

Despite the fact that he came from Burgundy, Felipe Vigarny adapted himself to the Spanish traditions and, together with Juan de Valmaseda and Diego Siloe, formed the group of artists who brought the Renaissance to Castile.

The altarpiece in the Royal Chapel at Granada (*see* Plate 1, black-and-white) is Vigarny's masterpiece. It was certainly the work of other great artists as well, such as Alonso Berruguete and Jacopo Florentino, whose Italian training is revealed in the stylistic innovations of the Renaissance which appear in their work. They may well have taken a hand in the designs and models for the altarpiece, for it is much ampler in its conception and more classical than Vigarny's other altars. It reveals traces of Michelangelo's style, particularly in the figures of the Evangelists, and although the ornament is poor in thematic material, it is wholly classical, being executed in what was then called the *Roman* style.

The polychromy was certainly the work of the two painters Antón de Plasencia and Alonso de Salamanca, who were working in the Chapel at the same time. The grotteschi are painted gold on black, the draperies are completely gilded and decorated with borders skilfully executed in *estofado* – the technique whereby the over-painting is hatched and scratched through to reveal the layer of gilt underneath.

The statue of *St Matthew* is situated in a right-hand register of the altarpiece. In its attitude it has affinities with Michelangelo's prophets in the Sistine Chapel, but none of their elegance. The evangelist is holding the book on his right knee and is turning to the left to dip his pen in the inkwell held by the kneeling angel.

The fact that this is the most outstanding of all Vigarny's altarpieces is due to its overall effect rather than to its individual figures. The composition is based on a series of large tableaux with figures projected in high relief, their dramatic effect heightened by the beauty of the polychromy.

II. ALONSO BERRUGUETE: THE ADORATION OF THE MAGI. FROM THE ALTAR OF SAN BENITO (DETAIL).

This relief is almost identical in its composition to that of Berruguete's painting for the altar of the Irish College in Salamanca. A comparison of the two works clearly shows that sculpture was Berruguete's real vocation. The painting, with its cold colouring, its conventional and careless execution, is only interesting as a proof of the freedom with which the artist interpreted Mannerist formulae, whereas the sculptural version of the same theme is vastly superior both for its originality of expression and its plasticity.

The *Adoration of the Magi* consists of figures carved almost in the round set against a high relief. The figures are approximately half life-size but are surprisingly disproportionate to one another. Berruguete seems to have been following the medieval convention of varying the size of each personage in relation to its importance. The scale of the figures is gradually reduced, from the Virgin and Child to St Joseph and the Magi: the standing St Joseph only reaches up to the level of the seated Virgin who is twice as large as the Magi. It is difficult to say whether this disproportion was due to any definite representative intention or aesthetic considerations, but although in the eyes of classicists it constituted a major defect, it did not affect the success of the composition.

The Virgin is seated in the centre of the composition which she dominates by her size and serenely majestic air. Her head shows a classic profile and her hair is fastened back with a ribbon as in the Florentine Madonnas. The Infant Christ is nude and chubby like one of Donatello's *putti* and appears excessively big for his age. The three Magi stand next to the absent-looking St Joseph and lack any royal attributes. They give the composition a dynamic sense of

movement with their violent gestures and restless bodies which can be seen through the clinging lines of their draperies.

The whole relief shines with gilt which is only slightly toned down in the background with small *graffito* decorations in black and narrow border ornamentation on the draperies. The warm glow of the gilt gives a metallic effect to the relief and transforms the humble wood into a material of magnificent sumptuousness.

III. JUAN DE JUNÍ: BURIAL OF CHRIST. SEGOVIA CATHEDRAL.

Juní's beautiful *Burial of Christ* in Segovia Cathedral has had the good fortune to be preserved in its chapel. It still stands in its original altar which is designed simply. Four Corinthian columns of classic grace contrast with the agitated movement of the sculpture and complement the effect of the great tragedy being enacted by the central group. This is placed between two warriors fighting between the columns, and below the figure of God the Father, in a circular niche bearing the date of the work: 1571.

Juan de Juní completed this work six years before his death and twenty-seven years after his other great version of the same theme in the convent of San Francisco, Valladolid. His earlier version was full of youthful expressive vigour and somewhat inclined to rhetoric and affectation, but in the Segovian *Burial of Christ,* made in his old age, his feeling had become more profound, and his technique purer. It is his masterpiece and can only be compared with his pathetic *Virgin of the Swords* which was doubtless made in the same period of his life.

The conception is rather of a lamentation than a burial. The body of Christ is stretched out naked on an altar cloth, worn-out and rigid – a figure of unsurpassable beauty. The surrounding group is treated like a relief and forms a single plastic unit comprising the figures of the Virgin, St John, the Magdalene, the other Mary, Joseph of Arimathea and Nicodemus. They are all reclining, sagging or collapsing to the ground, overcome by a grief that bears down on them like a crushing weight, preventing them from raising their heads. They give an almost tangible impression of overwhelming sorrow similar to that produced by the *Virgin of the Swords* at the foot of the Cross. Never before had Christian art attained such an effect of overwhelming pathos. With her extended arms the Virgin seems about to clasp the body of her Son in a loving embrace; St John holds out his hand to her as if to sustain her in her anguish, and the Magdalene bends over Christ's feet as though she lacks strength even to weep, so exhausted is she by her sorrow.

There is not a single discordant note in this harrowing composition. The grief of the figures is self-sustaining and free from all stridency, and the beauty of both features and attitudes is unimpaired. The richly detailed modelling is faultless; every figure is lovingly carved in smooth flowing lines and expressive planes, and Juní's expert technique is allied with an inspiration that it serves to the utmost.

The altar appears complete in every respect and the polychromy, white and gold for the architecture of the altar and delicately toned for the figures, has remained intact. The figures were painted according to the customs of the day with a burnishing technique: pale tints for the flesh parts, livid tones for the body of Christ, estofado for the draperies with delicately executed graffito ornamentation over the gilt. The colours are cold and include greyish-blues, pale yellows and deep crimsons. The name of the painter is not known but his art has strikingly enhanced this most majestic of all Juní's sculptures.

IV. GREGORIO FERNÁNDEZ: DEAD CHRIST. CAPU-CHIN MONASTERY, EL PARDO.

The date for this work was once mistakenly given as 1605, which would make it the first of Fernández's known works. Recently documentary evidence has advanced the date to 1614 in accordance with the style it displays, which is that of the artist's mature period. Despite the change of dating the work remains the prototype for all known succeeding versions. It was commissioned by Philip III who presented it to the Capuchin monastery of El Pardo where it has remained to this day.

Although some similar figures of prior date are in existence, they were all carved in the round as free-standing statues, such as the Christ in Las Descalzas Reales at Madrid, which is attributed to Gaspar Becerra, but the recumbent Christ on an altar-cloth separated from the scene of the Burial was Fernández's original iconographic innovation. Thus,

the traditional theme became replaced by a devotional image which was usually carried in religious processions in accordance with the rising cult of the Passion, a characteristic of the seventeenth century in Spain.

The effigy of the Dead Christ is shown lying on an altar-cloth with the head on a cushion decorated on its borders with popular Castilian themes. The body is naked except for a loin-cloth tied around the hips with a cord. The head is inclined on the right shoulder and the position of the legs is the same as that on the Cross, with the left slightly bent. There is an open wound in the side of the body with streaks of coagulated blood.

The anatomical structure is gently stressed by the modelling and is inspired by realism rather than classical formulas, attaining maximum perfection and beauty. The emotion produced by the body is purely plastic and is most concentrated in the head but its expression is free from all violent strivings after effect or facile melodramatic touches. The features have purity and nobility, the hair and beard hang in curling strands, and the eyes and mouth are half open as though to express an exhausted suffering after the terrible ordeal of the Crucifixion.

Although Fernández did not paint his sculptures himself, he made a point of supervising the polychroming to ensure that it enhanced the effect of the carving. The polychromy of the Dead Christ has remained intact: white for the draperies, light brown for the body and black for the hair. The technique used was the same as that for easel paintings with the use of a matt oil tint which was then polished to give an enamel effect, in contrast to the estofado of the sixteenth century, strengthening the naturalism of the sculpture. This Dead Christ is perhaps Fernández's most beautiful work and represents the fusion of the most refined plasticity with the profoundest religious feeling.

V. MANUEL PEREYRA: SAINT BRUNO. CHARTER-HOUSE OF MIRAFLORES, BURGOS.

The Portuguese Manuel Pereyra was born in Oporto in 1588 and came to Castile in search of greater opportunities to practise his art. He went to Madrid, which was then also the capital of Portugal, attracting artists from far and wide to its Court, and became a sculptor of the first rank. He died there in 1683, old and blind, but covered in riches, fame and honours.

Pereyra's vein of Portuguese lyricism was subdued by the prevailing mood of realism in art, but the crudities of an excessive realism in his work are always modified by his good taste. Like the painter Zurbarán, he was a conventual sculptor, as is proved by the sincerity and restraint of his images. His most famous work of all is the *St Bruno* in the charterhouse of Miraflores at Burgos, in the chapel of the saint on the left of the church. The statue was given to the church by Cardinal Zapata who died in 1635, thus giving us an approximate date for the work which belongs to the artist's first period at Madrid, before he was influenced by Alonso Cano.

Pereyra conceived the saint as a living person rather than as an abstract ideal. The statue was not derived from any model but was created according to the artist's own conception of the personality of the founder-saint of the Carthusian order, as a man full of energy as well as inner life. He is ascetic rather than contemplative with a lean face tanned by the open air and the sun, and modelled by the intense spirituality which is revealed in his ardent gaze. The head is so full of life that it has been said that it would speak, were it not a Carthusian.

The saint is shown with a tonsured head and wearing a white habit with thick, vertical folds, and his features are admirably naturalistic. His gaze is fixed on the crucifix in his hand and his attitude is a triumph of realism enhanced by a masterly polychromy. The painter was probably Francisco Camilo who frequently collaborated with Pereyra.

A work of art can immortalize reality. In the case of Pereyra's *St Bruno* it brings a piece of ordinary wood to life with such vividness that the observer is no longer sure whether he is seeing a man-made image or a living being turned to wood.

VI. JUAN MARTÍNEZ MONTAÑÉS: CHRIST OF CLEMENCY. SEVILLE CATHEDRAL.

On Corpus Christi day, 1602, the vain and worldly Archdeacon of Carmona, Mateo Vázquez de Leca, was following a veiled lady through the streets of Seville. When he caught up with her, so the story goes, she unveiled herself and Vázquez found himself confronted by a skeleton. As a result of this vision he underwent a veritable conversion: he tried to become a Carthusian monk but was opposed in this by the Cathedral Chapter, of which he was a member as the chaplain for the Chapel of the Chalices, and he spent the rest of his life in exemplary virtue.

On 5th April in the following year he commissioned Montañés to make a Crucifix for his private oratory, probably by way of expiation for his sins. The contract stipulated that the image of Christ should be "alive before His death, with His head hanging over his chest, looking down at any who might be praying at His feet, as though Christ Himself were speaking to them and were lamenting that His sufferings were for whomever should be praying to Him, and thus should have a certain severity in His eyes and features, and the eyes wide open". Montañés promised that the image would be "executed and finished by my own hand and with the greatest perfection", and although the price of the work was fixed at 300 ducats, he offered to make it worth 500 ducats, declaring that "I make a free gift of it to the said archdeacon of Carmona for I have a great desire to make a similar image so that it will stay in Spain and not be taken to the Indies or any other part of the world, and that the client who made it for the glory of God may be known". The archdeacon's piety and Montañés's proposal to immortalize his name resulted in the creation of one of the master works of Spanish religious sculpture which is now the pride of Seville Cathedral, where it may be seen in the Sanctuary of the Chalices.

The image of Christ is, therefore, an unusual one. He was traditionally shown either dead or, less frequently, as about to die with His head facing upwards, but Montañés's Christ is represented looking downwards at the worshippers by the foot of the Cross. The image is carved in cedar wood, as was customary in Andalusia for very special works. The body is completely naturalistic and extremely beautiful: the modelling of the anatomy is perfect and demonstrates Montañés's effort to interpret the theme of "the most beautiful of all the sons of Man" as worthily as possible rather than to establish a new canon for the sculptor's art. Following the pattern created by Pacheco, Montañés depicted Christ on the Cross with four nails. It had been customary in Spanish art to represent Christ on the Cross with the legs parallel and the feet nailed to a foot-support, but Montañés chose a more artistic attitude which he derived from a number of Sevillian crucifixes influenced by a bronze *Christ* from Italy, which had been supposedly cast from one of Michelangelo's models. The *Christ of Clemency* is shown with the legs crossed and the feet are fastened by two nails driven directly into the wood of the Cross. The draperies are cut in a mass of folds and are knotted around the hips without interrupting the downward flow of the body's lines.

The polychromy was carried out by Montañés's friend and habitual colleague Francisco Pacheco, who later cited this process as an example of how flesh parts should be painted when he wrote his treatise on painting. He recommended a technique similar to that used for oil paintings on canvas: the use of oils over specially primed wood and a gradation of tones to obtain a naturalistic effect. Pacheco's colours for the *Christ of Clemency* are the same as those used by Velázquez for his painting of the *Crucifixion*: light brown for the body, black for the hair, and white for the drapery.

The emotion produced by the figure is due entirely to the head which faces downwards with a half-open mouth as if it were about to speak. The expression is rather one of gentle sadness at Man's cruelty than one of severity. Montañés seems to have been inspired by the archdeacon's spirit of repentance when he created this sublime *Crucifixion* which recalls the lines of Lope de Vega's moving *Soneto*:

> "Oye, pastor, pues por amores mueres...
> Espera, pues, y escucha mis cuidados.
> Pero ¿como te digo que me esperes
> si estás para esperar los pies clavados?" [1]

VII. JUAN DE MESA: THE CHRIST OF GREAT POWER (DETAIL). CHURCH OF SAN LORENZO, SEVILLE.

Every Holy Thursday in Seville, a devout crowd of worshippers congregates in the *plaza* in front of the Church of San Lorenzo to await the chimes of midnight. At midnight the church doors swing open and a long file of hooded penitents emerges, followed by the *Christ of Great Power* carried in procession. To the hushed crowd the statue seems almost alive when seen in the light of the flickering candles and the moon, as if it were conveying its grief to the multitude around it. The mounting tension is broken at last by the pathetic notes of a *saeta* cutting through the silence – the climax of Holy Week in Seville. Juan de Mesa endowed his great statue with an unrivalled degree of pathos: seen in its niche in the chapel it is impressive enough, but when brought outside the church, the impression it produces is one of high tragedy, terrifying in its impact.

Mesa received the commission for this work in 1620, shortly after Montañés had scored such a striking success with his *Christ of the Passion,* an *imagen de vestir,* representing Christ carrying the Cross. Although this was the only processional image that Montañés ever made, Juan de Mesa made a speciality of this type of work. This was probably due to the exigencies of the confraternities who wanted the finest workmanship at the least expense.

There is no doubt that Montañés's statue served as the model for that of Mesa and, moreover, the theme had already been treated earlier by Ocampo and Pablo de Rojas. The *Christ of Great Power* is larger than life-size and only the body and articulated arms are carved, the rest being covered with a real costume as in Montañés's version of the same attitude: Christ is shown walking with his head inclined towards the right. But there the resemblance ends, for Montañés's Christ has an anguished beauty combined with a depth of inner feeling, while Mesa's statue displays a pathos that is both frightening and violent.

Long curling strands of hair on the Christ's head seem to be matted with sweat and blood, the mouth is gaping with exhaustion and the veins of the neck stand out prominently. The finely carved feet and hands show the tendons tensed with effort. The crown of thorns was added later to Montañés's statue, but here it is carved in the same wood, as is usual in Mesa's Crucifixions. The dark tones of the crown seem to be due rather to the patina of the walnut than to any polychromy.

It is only in Juan de Mesa's work that Andalusian sculpture attains such dramatic intensity of emotion. Mesa may have repeated the same themes and artistic formulae as Montañés, but he shows a quite different temperament. In Montañés's sculpture suffering is transformed and softened into serenity; the grief of Mesa's statues is intensified and overflowing.

---

[1] "Hear, Shepherd, Thou who for Thy flock art dying...
Oh, wait! to Thee my weary soul is crying,
Wait for me: yet why ask it, when I see,
With feet nailed to the cross, Thou'rt waiting still for me!"
Translated by Henry Wadsworth Longfellow

VIII. ALONSO CANO: THE IMMACULATE CON-
CEPTION. GRANADA CATHEDRAL.

See note for Plate 64

IX. ALONSO CANO: HEAD OF SAINT JOHN OF
GOD. MUSEUM OF FINE ARTS, GRANADA.

This head formerly belonged to an *imagen de vestir*.
This was one of the statues which were specially
designed to be clothed with real costumes; they first
appeared in medieval times and were a characteristic
of seventeenth-century art in Spain. Although such
statues were sometimes carved throughout, the parts
that were to be draped were usually left unfinished.
As a general rule the sculptor confined himself to
carving the head and extremities, leaving the rest of
the figure as a kind of armature for the costume;
many of these statues were made, on account of
their cheapness, and it was to one of these that the
head of *St John of God* seems to have belonged.

Its excellence of execution has caused it to be
attributed to Cano, for only he or his best pupil,
Pedro de Mena, could have carved such a head, but
its realism is too great for Mena to have made it.
The features also have a slightly melancholic expression that was characteristic of Cano but not of his
pupil. Similarly the fine polychromy could only be
the work of Cano who, as is known, was a painter in
his own right and accustomed to painting his own
statues.

The cult of St John of God was mainly confined to
Granada where he was deeply venerated. It was there
that the Portuguese adventurer had come after his
conversion by St John of Avila to start his sublime career of charitable works, founding the Order
of the Brotherhood of Hospitallers, delivering up his
soul to God and leaving his body to be venerated by
the local inhabitants of the city. He was represented
in sculptures and paintings after 1630 when he was
canonised. Cano's head of St John was therefore one of
the many images of the saint made for his veneration.

The head bears a close resemblance to that in the
portrait attributed to Pedro Raxis, the best painter
in Granada at the close of the sixteenth century, who
depicted the saint more or less according to tradition.
Although Cano had painted very few portraits as
far as we know, he showed himself exceptionally
gifted in this, his only portrait sculpture. Instead of

following his usual tendency to idealize reality, he
managed to give a strongly individual character to
this head. The carving is vigorous and restrained:
the features are those of a man of great will-power,
disposed to action but with a certain melancholy in
his pensive eyes. The polychromy is executed with
Cano's habitual perfection and emphasizes the
expressive power of the carving. The saint is shown
with short brown hair, a thin moustache, clean-
shaven chin and eyes made of glass. The use of glass
for the eyes became frequent in sculpture from about
the middle of the seventeenth century and adds
greatly to the realism of Cano's astounding portrait.

The provenance of the head is unknown. It is
one of many works of art that were removed from
convents after the secularization laws for church
property were passed in 1836. It was acquired by
the Museum of Fine Arts at Granada.

X. PEDRO DE MENA: SAINT FRANCIS. TOLEDO
CATHEDRAL.

In 1653 Pedro de Mena was appointed sculptor for
Toledo Cathedral. His appointment was probably
due to the satisfaction he had given to the cathedral
Chapter with his statue of St Francis which they had
commissioned, and which is now in the Treasury
of the cathedral. The work has been attributed to
Mena since the eighteenth century, although some
modern opinion has put forward the name of Cano.
The style is entirely Mena's but it is extremely
probable that the model for the statue was in fact
Cano's creation.

The statue is half life-size, carved in cedar-wood
and the eyes are made of glass. Its beautiful polychromy has survived intact. The saint is standing
stiffly erect, head raised, eyes upturned, a hood round
his head, and hands hidden in the linked sleeves of
his habit, which is carved in deep vertical folds with
only one foot showing. His appearance tallies with
the fifteenth-century account of how the Pope
Nicholas V was dazzled by the vision of the undecayed
body of the saint standing over his tomb at Assisi as
it was about to be opened.

That the statue was inspired by a similar work by
Cano, now lost, is of no importance in the appreci-
ation of Mena's version. Its powerful effect and the
feeling it arouses could only come from the hand of
genius. Mena's representation of the saint's body is

confined to the head and the tip of one foot; the remainder of the statue consists of a habit with a minimum of folds to suggest the lines of the body, which is little more than a support for the head. The features are almost fleshless, the facial muscles are tensed over the cheeks, the ecstatic eyes are deeply sunk and the mouth half open. The rounded hood frames the face and acts as a halo. All life seems to have left the figure as if the saint had turned to stone after his ecstatic soul had rushed out of his body to soar up to Heaven.

The realism of the statue was not derived from any actual model but was inspired by Mena's own personal vision of the saint. It required more imagination to create a reality outside normal experience than to give form to dehumanized fantasies. Never before had an artist been so fired by the divine spark of creation.

XI. JOSÉ DE MORA: DOLOROSA. CONVENT OF LAS MARAVILLAS, MADRID.

José de Mora was the interpreter *par excellence* of the theme of *pena,* that kind of grief which is peculiar to the people of Andalusia and, in particular, Granada. *Pena* is a silent affliction, a hidden noiseless grief which takes possession of body and soul, which cannot be communicated, and is beyond all consolation. It can produce a certain feeling of bitter enjoyment in those afflicted by it who gauge the extent of their sufferings by the depth of their particular *pena.* Mora's Dolorosas seem to be telling us: "This great suffering is mine alone. Nothing can take it from me for nothing can comprehend it. Leave me alone with my grief for it is my only companion."

The *Dolorosa* in the Carmelite convent of Las Maravillas at Madrid is one of a pair of figures. The other, as was customary, is an *Ecce Homo* which suffers from an excessive languidity and is much less interesting. Both are half-length figures which are a speciality of Mora's work. They were probably made in Madrid for a commission obtained by Mora when he was living at the Court, which would suggest they are his first versions of this theme. Both the figures have remained intact in their carving and their polychromy, all by Mora's own hand.

This *Dolorosa* is the earliest in the whole series. As in Mora's bust for the Granadine convent at Zafra, the Virgin seems rather to be mourning Christ's death, than stricken by the presentiment of His suffering. Her head is slightly inclined and full of sorrow but appears to be a stylized portrait of Mora's wife. Her features appear constantly in Mora's sculptures for she was the great love of his life and it was her death that brought on the artist's madness. The *Dolorosa's* face is light-brown, framed by dark straight-flowing hair, the eyes are half shut and tears are slowly coursing down her cheeks while her mouth seems to quiver with a repressed sob. She is wearing a crimson-violet tunic with a low neckline, and a light blue mantle draped over her head and falling over her shoulders in shallow folds.

Mora's carving is characteristically sober and unobtrusive with delicate suggestions of *chiaroscuro* in its intonations. Glass eyes and tears have been used with such discretion that they are hardly noticeable. The soft tones of the polychromy are in perfect harmony with the gentle and intimate character of the image.

XII. PEDRO ROLDÁN: BURIAL OF CHRIST. HOSPITAL DE LA CARIDAD, SEVILLE.

See note for Plates 81-88

NOTES ON THE MONOCHROME PLATES

1. FELIPE VIGARNY DE BORGOÑA: RELIEF IN THE ALTAR OF THE ROYAL CHAPEL, GRANADA (DETAIL).

This relief is found on the predella of the main altar in the Royal Chapel and is a detail from the scene of the surrender of Granada and the baptism of the Moors. Although no documents relating to the altar have been found it was attributed to Felipe Vigarny by Bermúdez de Pedraza, the historian of Granada, in 1602. This statement tallies with Vigarny's documented stay in the city in 1521 when he was working in the Chapel, two years after he had entered a partnership with Alonso Berruguete to work in Granada. Although the contract was to last for four years we do not know if it was fulfilled.

Felipe Vigarny, or Felipe de Borgoña as he was called, was born in Langres in the Champagne district. In 1498 he was already working on a series of large reliefs in the Cathedral and went to Toledo, Salamanca and Palencia before arriving in Granada. Of all his works his altar in the Royal Chapel is the most original and comes closest to the spirit of the Renaissance. Vigarny may have been influenced by Domenico Fancelli's tomb of the Catholic kings in the Chapel, by Berruguete's work as a painter, and also by his colleagues, Jacopo Florentino and Pedro Machuca. All these artists were exponents of the Italian style and none of them had previously been connected with Vigarny.

The portion of the relief illustrated shows the procession of the victorious Christian besiegers on their way to the gates of Granada to receive the keys of the city from Boabdil. The mounted figures of the Catholic monarchs, Ferdinand and Isabella, are shown in the foreground, with the Archbishop of Toledo on their right, and the Count Tendilla on their left. Immediately behind them is a group of noblemen and ladies, including the princess Doña Isabel, and the rear is brought up by a band of infantrymen with halberds marching in close formation. Vigarny always paid a great deal of attention to the features of the personages he represented, and it seems certain that his figure of the archbishop is really a portrait of Cardinal Cisneros, instead of the Cardinal Mendoza who was present at the taking of Granada.

This may have been Vigarny's way of paying homage to the memory of the Cardinal who had recently died. Cisneros was responsible for his commission to carve the altar in Toledo Cathedral between 1502 and 1504 and he had already been portrayed by Vigarny during his lifetime. Although the King ordered Vigarny to change the features of the Cardinal in the relief the order was never carried out.

The general composition of the relief is somewhat medieval. Vigarny's style marks a transition from the Gothic to the Italianate in his realistic treatment of features, costumes and attitudes, and his decorative sense is entirely Italianate. The grandeur and opulence of the subject is enhanced by a rich polychromy of gilt and *estofado* which was probably the work of Antón de Plasencia and Alonso de Salamanca.

2-6. JACOPO FLORENTINO (JACOMÉ FLORENTÍN): BURIAL OF CHRIST. MUSEUM OF FINE ARTS, GRANADA.

The magnificent *Burial of Christ,* formerly in the monastery of San Jerónimo, Granada, is a striking example of the way in which Spanish art assimilated foreign elements in its finest periods. In view of its almost Gothic simplicity, its intimate air of pathos and the traditional polychromed wood in which it is carved, it comes as a surprise to learn that its sculptor was an Italian and, moreover, one of Michelangelo's colleagues.

Jacopo Florentino (also called Torni 'L'Indaco' in Italy) was a native of Florence and had helped Michelangelo in his paintings for the Sistine Chapel. He was known only as a painter in Italy but when he came to Spain he also practised sculpture and architecture. He came to Granada in 1520, probably direct from Italy, with two Spaniards – the architect and painter Pedro Machuca, and the painter and sculptor Alonso Berruguete, with whom he was to work in the Royal Chapel. Late in life he married the daughter of a sculptor from Jaen and died in 1526 without having returned to Italy.

His surviving work includes an *Annunciation* in the doorway of the sacristy of the Royal Chapel, several figures in the doorway of the sacristy of Murcia Cathedral, whose tower he also began, and a number of wood carvings, among them an impressive *Crucifixion* for the convent of San Agustín and the group here illustrated. Despite lack of documentation, the attribution of these works to Jacopo has never been questioned.

We do not know the original destination for this group of figures. It may have been intended for one of the altars designed for the transept of the Royal Chapel which was never completed, and the earliest known site of the work was in an altar with plaster decorations in the Plateresque style in the cloister of the monastery of San Jerónimo. When the monastery was secularized this group was removed first to the church and finally to the museum where it was installed in a facsimile of the original altarpiece.

The theme of this work had already been treated in a similar manner, and in a style of restrained realism, by northern European and particularly French artists from Gothic times to the early Renaissance. In comparison with their work there is nothing archaic about Jacopo's interpretation: the sarcophagus is covered with elegant vegetal ornamentation in the traditional Florentine manner, the body of Christ shows a profound knowledge of anatomy and classical proportions, and the influence of the *Laocoön* group is evident in the heads of St John and Nicodemus. Although Jacopo made use of Renaissance elements in this work, his style has nothing in common with that of Michelangelo. It seems as though he had deliberately kept himself out of the aura of attraction that surrounded Michelangelo and which had fascinated so many other artists – Italian and foreign alike. Jacopo had surrendered to his new environment and developed his art according to the Spanish tradition. It was not only his craftsmanship that became hispanicized, with his use of polychromy and gilt; the way in which he gave such an intense religious feeling to his work was also quite un-Italian.

The fundamental impression produced by this work is one of serenity tinged with profound pathos. The composition is almost symmetrical: centring upon the horizontal body of the Dead Christ framed by the slightly curving figures of St Joseph and Nicodemus, richly apparelled in a Judaic style. The four statues of the Virgin, St John and the two Marys are united in a symmetrical movement. The figure on the extreme left, that of Maria Salome huddled in grief beneath her mantle, is especially fine, but the attitude of the Virgin is less original. With her inclined head and suffering gesture she is the typical Virgin at the foot of the Cross seen so often in Gothic art. As mentioned already, the influence of the *Laocoön* group is manifest in the statue of St John, especially in the way he expresses his grief with upturned eyes and open mouth. Even the treatment of his hair is derived from the famous Hellenistic sculpture, which created a sensation among Italian artists when it was discovered late in the fifteenth century. The most original statue in the whole group is that of the Magdalene. The conception is one of delicacy and emotion, while the way she is holding her long, flowing hair is in keeping with medieval art. Nicodemus's face is a free rendering of the main figure in the *Laocoön* and contrasts with Joseph of Arimathea's aquiline features which seem to be a portrayal from life, perhaps of Jacopo himself who was described by his son as being 'tall, lean and spare of countenance'.

The exquisite polychromy is by Antón de Plasencia. He used the *estofado* technique, first gilding the draperies and even the Magdalene's hair, then painting over the gilt with very fine brush strokes, making decorative border patterns in the Renaissance style.

7. PIETRO TORRIGIANI: SAINT JEROME. MUSEUM OF FINE ARTS, SEVILLE.

Pietro Torrigiani was another Florentine artist who came to Spain in the early sixteenth century. He had been a sculptor at the court of the Medici and had fled from Florence as a result of his famous quarrel with Michelangelo whose nose he had smashed, disfiguring him for life. He had been a soldier, worked at Rome, and fought bravely in the battle of Garigliano before going to England where he became Royal Sculptor to Henry VII, winning fame and fortune before moving on to Spain in about 1525. His adventurous life ended in disaster when he was denounced as a heretic by the Duke of Arcos for breaking a statue of the Virgin after a dispute about payment. He died, aged fifty-six, on a hunger strike in the dungeons of the Inquisition in 1528.

Although Torrigiani had also worked in stone and bronze, his Spanish works were all made in terracotta. Only two of these figures can definitively be attributed to him: the *St Jerome* and the *Virgin and Child* which are both in Seville Museum. However, a similar *Virgin and Child* in the University Chapel and another terracotta *St Jerome* in the monastery at Guadelupe are traditionally ascribed to him and indeed are not unworthy of his hand.

Polychrome terracotta sculpture had been a traditional Sevillian art ever since Mercadante had used the medium for his statues and reliefs for the side doors of the façade of the cathedral. Torrigiani also modelled busts in the Flemish and Florentine manner both in England and in Spain, but his statues in the Museum are his only known large terracotta figures.

Torrigiani's penitent figure of *St Jerome*, which formerly belonged to the monastery at Benavista before its dissolution, is deservedly his most famous work. In this statue the artist shows himself to be far removed from Jacopo Florentino's delicacy of feeling and religious intensity, for his work was always deliberately frigid, impassive and disciplined. His *St Jerome* might almost have been conceived as a lesson in anatomical structure for the benefit of later sculptors in Seville and elsewhere. Far from representing the wasted body of a penitent the statue is heavily muscled and well rounded and is almost boring in its perfection. It was certainly not conceived as an example of the classical ideal of beauty that had become conventional and popularly accepted in sixteenth-century Italy, for it is a representation of a real, living human body. With its naturalism enhanced by polychromy it is the result of observation from life allied to a scientific study of anatomy.

8-11. BARTOLOMÉ ORDÓÑEZ: TOMB OF JOAN THE MAD AND PHILIP THE HANDSOME. ROYAL CHAPEL, GRANADA.

In 1518 Charles V had commissioned Domenico Fancelli to build a tomb for his parents, King Philip and Queen Joan, which was to be situated next to the artist's previous work, the tomb of the Catholic monarchs, in the Royal Chapel at Granada. When Fancelli died that same year the contract was given to a Spanish sculptor, Bartolomé Ordóñez of Burgos, who had trained in Italy, perhaps in Fancelli's own studio.

Ordóñez was already known at the time for his work in Naples and in the choir of Barcelona Cathedral, but the royal tomb was the most important work

of his career. He moved his workshop from Barcelona to Carrara in Italy to begin working on the tomb, when he suddenly died in 1520. His known activity lasted for only three years, but within this short time he had almost completed the royal tomb and half finished two others, for Cardinal Cisneros and the Fonseca family, apart from his earlier mentioned work.

Ordóñez was the Spanish sculptor who came closest to the spirit of the Italian Renaissance. He worked only in marble, except for the wooden panels in the Barcelona choir-stalls, and completely assimilated the Italian style except for its pagan worship of form. Where he differs from the Italian artists is in his profound religious feeling, his purity and his attention to the theme represented. Despite his Italianate style he was always a Castilian at heart.

Ordóñez altered Fancelli's original design for the royal tomb by raising a casket for the sarcophagus over the catafalque and by making the walls vertical. The corners are flanked by royal emblems and grotesque figures holding naked infants in their claws. The masculine figures at the head of the tomb hold the chain and the fleece which were emblems of the Order of the Fleece of which Philip had been Grand Master, while at the foot of the tomb the female figures display a yoke and a bundle of arrows, attributes inherited by Queen Joan from her parents, Ferdinand and Isabella. The catafalque itself is decorated with vaulted niches containing figures of the Virtues, and medallions with biblical scenes: the Nativity, the Adoration of the Kings, the Sermon on the Mount and the Burial of Christ. All four medallions are carved in high relief and are beautifully composed, but they are also in lower relief than was customary in Ordóñez's work. They are so finely carved that they fully justify Francisco de Holanda's opinion of the artist, who was one of his "Four Eagles", as being "excellent in bas-relief".

The casket is raised over the catafalque and bears the recumbent effigies of the King and Queen, both beautifully idealized.

Around the casket their armorial shields and epitaph are upheld by cherubs and angels and the corners are flanked by statues of their patron saints, St Andrew and St Michael of Burgundy and the two SS John of Castile. Only SS John the Baptist and Andrew are by Ordóñez's own hand for the others were unfinished at his death and were completed by his pupils. The statue of St John is extremely fine with its realistic rendering of vigorous male anatomy, which comes closer to the art of Donatello than that of Michelangelo. In the figure of St Andrew, Ordóñez displayed his skill in carving drapery with elegance and simplicity. Both statues are strikingly original and well composed. The rest of the decoration consists of a profusion of exquisitely carved ornamental motifs including garlands of fruit and beautiful foliage ornaments in the Tuscan style. The tomb is certainly the richest example of funerary art in the whole of the Renaissance, including even Italy. In its originality and beauty it excels Fancelli's tomb beside it, and it is an eloquent witness to Ordóñez's skill and fine decorative sense.

When Ordóñez died the tomb was brought from Carrara by his pupils, but as Queen Joan was still living it was not placed in the chapel. It was kept in storage where some of the figures were damaged, and was only brought out in 1602 when it was finally set beside Fancelli's tomb for the Catholic monarchs. By then the Renaissance was over and with it the opportunity for the tomb to influence the Spanish sculptors of its time.

12 and 13. DIEGO SILOE: DEAD CHRIST. CHAPEL OF THE CONSTABLE, BURGOS CATHEDRAL.

The sumptuous Chapel of the Constable was built at the end of the fifteenth century by the Constable of Castile, Don Diego de Velasco, and its altars were completed when the Renaissance was at its height. The first altar, dedicated to St Anne, was commissioned to the fine late Gothic sculptor Gil Siloe who died before he could complete it. The figures were completed by his son Diego, who made the beautiful group of the *Dead Christ* being supported by two angels.

After working in Naples as a young man with his compatriot, Bartolomé Ordóñez, Diego Siloe had returned to Burgos. He became one of the major figures in Spanish Renaissance art, both as a sculptor and architect, working mainly in Burgos and Granada, where he directed the building of the cathedral. There is nothing in his work to remind one of his father, for he was perfectly at home in the new style, although he followed it less closely than Ordóñez and kept up the traditional use of polychromed wood, besides working in stone and marble.

Diego Siloe's *Dead Christ* is a youthful work. The theme is Italian and one rarely encountered in Spanish art but Siloe's interpretation of it is highly original. The body of Christ is modelled with a feeling for realism rather than the classical tradition and is shown being supported by two wingless angels of female appearance who betray their grief by their gestures. The polychromy, the work of León Picardo, harmonizes perfectly with the carving. It consists of delicate grotesques in *graffito* for the draperies and almost matt tints for the flesh parts.

14. DIEGO SILOE: SAINT JEROME. CHAPEL OF THE CONSTABLE, BURGOS CATHEDRAL.

Siloe's *St Jerome* was carved for the altar of St Peter which he made jointly with Vigarny, with whom he also collaborated on the main altar. Although the altar of St Peter was designed as a companion piece to that of St Anne, it was carved in the Plateresque, as opposed to the other's Gothic style.

Siloe's saint resembles Torrigiani's *St Jerome,* but he could not have been influenced by it as there is no evidence to show that he was in Andalusia while Torrigiani was working there. The theme had first been treated in painting, both in Flanders and in Italy, but it did not appear in sculpture until the sixteenth century. Siloe's work was the first of its kind to be seen in Castile and was later widely imitated. The saint is represented in his grotto at Bethlehem where he did penance while he translated the Holy Scriptures. He is shown half-kneeling on the rocks, gazing at the crucifix with an anguished expression and about to beat his chest with a stone. A lion is reclining under the crucifix as the saint's characteristic attribute and also as a symbol for the desert. The statue is about half life-size and carved completely in the round, although it was set in a vaulted niche in the altarpiece.

Although Siloe had taken pains to show the saint in the greatest anatomical exactitude, as an old man complete with wrinkled skin, he was just as concerned to bring out the spiritual content of his subject. The saint's tortured expression and the way he seems to be about to fall swooning on the rocks are evidence of his inner struggle in his endeavour to overcome evil with divine help in front of the image of Christ. We have come a long way from the frigidity of the classical style. Siloe was one of the most impassioned and emotional sculptors of the Spanish Renaissance and more than a century ahead of his time in his realism.

15. DIEGO SILOE: THE SCOURGING OF CHRIST. BURGOS MUSEUM (DETAIL).

Siloe's realism and pathos can also be appreciated in his *Scourging of Christ* and the *Ecce Homo,* prototypes of the processional images, or *pasos* as they were called, of the seventeenth century. Siloe did not use his theme as a pretext to show his bravura in modelling a male nude, but rather to bring out all the inherent emotion of the subject. The statue illustrated is life-size. The posture of the figure now seems strange and hard to explain, but that is because the column to which it was originally attached has disappeared. The head, with its suggestion of suffering and exhaustion, is extremely moving. The thick curling hair hanging loosely down and away from the head is characteristic of Siloe's figures. The polychromy contributes to the dramatic effect of the statue by emphasizing the red and livid weals left by the scourge.

Siloe made a similar statue in his *Ecce Homo* in the church of Dueñas, Burgos, which has a crown of thorns and a purple mantle, and he repeated the theme in the main altar of the Constable's Chapel. However Siloe did not only strive for dramatic effect for, unlike his contemporary Berruguete, his female and child figures are always distinguished by softness and refinement of handling. His Madonnas were the most influential of their time and were widely imitated by other figure sculptors.

16. DIEGO SILOE: SAINT JOHN THE BAPTIST. NATIONAL MUSEUM OF SCULPTURE, VALLADOLID.

This panel was part of the Abbot's choir-stall in the monastery of San Benito at Valladolid. We do not know the history of the choir-stalls, but the fact that Siloe only carved this and two other reliefs for the stalls seems to indicate that they were only done as examples, as was the custom in such cases, and that for an unknown reason the whole commission was then given to an inferior artist. The stalls are said to have been begun in 1522 and were being completed in 1528.

This relief is carved in plain walnut-wood and shows Siloe's mastery in carving and polishing for the panel has an almost jewel-like finish. Although Siloe rivalled Ordóñez, he did not share the latter's predilection for composed scenes, preferring to carve isolated figures which provided the best vehicle for his talents. The carving of the saint is perfect: there is nothing excessive and nothing is lacking. The book symbolizes the saint's prophetic mission and the lamb is a reminder of the saint's words on recognizing Christ as the Messiah: "Behold, the Lamb of God." The carving of the torso and the heap of stone slabs show Siloe's style at its finest.

Siloe only reveals his Italian training in his mastery of form and his outstanding decorative sense. All his work is suffused with a depth of feeling that ranges from the dramatic to the tender and restrained, and spiritual intensity is combined with a purity of form that never plagiarizes or copies from Italian art. The borders of the panel are decorated with classical grotesques, but the originality of his ornamentation led to the formation of a whole school and enables one to trace his influence in Castile and even in Andalusia.

17. ALONSO BERRUGUETE: PROPHET. FROM THE ALTAR OF SAN BENITO. NATIONAL MUSEUM OF SCULPTURE, VALLADOLID.

Berruguete's altarpiece for the monastery of San Benito at Valladolid has sealed his reputation as a sculptor in modern times. He was the son of the painter Pedro Berruguete and was born at Paredes de Nava near Palencia; he went to Italy as a youth to study painting there. On his return to Spain he trained in the midst of a group of artists who had gathered around the young King Charles V in the hope that he would be a new Maecenas. After their hopes were dashed Berruguete turned from painting to sculpture, to the benefit of Spanish art, for it was here that he found his true vocation. His first altar, for the monastery at La Mejorada, may be criticized for certain defects, but the altar for San Benito in Valladolid is one of the finest of the period.

The structural design of the altarpiece, its paintings, figures and polychromy are all Berruguete's own work. He obtained the contract in 1526 but only began work in about 1528 completing it in 1533. At first the judges for the finished work, among whom was

Vigarny, wanted Berruguete to make various alterations but they finally accepted the work as it stood. They based their objections upon the fact that Berruguete's technique was faulty, probably because he had not undergone a serious apprenticeship. Being the son of a painter and a painter himself Berruguete was incapable of visualising form without colour. His polychromy and the pieces of stiffened cloth he placed over the figures hid the faults of his carving and detracted somewhat from the basic sculptural qualities of his work.

Berruguete's carvings for the altar consist of sculptures in the round and reliefs. His largest figures are those of *St Benedict,* the *Assumption,* and the *Calvary,* the others being about a third of life-size. They include prophets, apostles and various saints of whom the majority are unidentifiable since they have no attributes. Together they made up a marvellous collection of characters and attitudes only surpassed by Michelangelo's prophets and young men in the Sistine Chapel.

The figure of a prophet is one of the finest. He is represented lifting his face up to heaven as if to receive divine inspiration and from his position, with his feet close together, he seems to be about to leap heavenwards in his ecstasy. The shape of his body is emphasized by the close-clinging draperies with gold and blue polychromy over a ground of burnished gilt. The emotion in the statue is not confined to the face, for the tense, concentrated posture of the body is full of a dynamic force expressing itself in spirit rather than in movement.

18 and 19. BERRUGUETE: HEADS OF TWO APOS-
TLES. FROM THE ALTAR OF SAN BENITO.

These two figures are generally supposed to be apostles because of the books they are holding. The first leans forward in a strange and unsteady posture with an expression of deep thought suggested by his knit brows and half-open mouth. The modelling of the face is lively and delicate, the hair curls in spirals and the beard is carved in loosely falling strands. The striking individuality of the whole head is due to the sculptor's imagination rather than being taken from life. In contrast to Michelangelo, Berruguete never made his faces impassive, they always confirm the emotion suggested by the attitudes of the bodies.

The second head has a very different expression,

full of pathos and suffering. The apostle seems to be crying out with the anguish that is ravaging his whole body. The carving is summary, as though Berruguete were working in a sudden fit of tormented inspiration, concentrating on the facial expression, and only roughly sketching the hair and the beard.

Both statues were made to be placed in gilded niches in the altarpiece at a distance from the onlooker but were not designed with a view to the whole. Instead they are the result of the artist's sudden inspiration and, since the altarpiece was dismantled, can now be studied at close quarters as they deserve.

20 and 21. BERRUGUETE: SAINT SEBASTIAN.
FROM THE ALTAR OF SAN BENITO.

Berruguete's statue of *St Sebastian* is one of his greatest and most popular works. In Christian iconography this theme had always given artists a pretext for painting or sculpting a young and beautiful male nude. Another subject which required the representation of male nudity was the Crucifixion, but its religious and dramatic implications prevented artists from indulging their delight in pure form, whereas the former theme gave them full liberty to do so. The interpretation of male nudity in art can thus be studied through its iconography.

Berruguete's *St Sebastian* is still almost an adolescent youth. The finely modelled body has a delicacy and an anatomical correctness that was rare in the artist's work. The statue proves that the spirit of the Renaissance with its love of human beauty sometimes found its way into the austere Castilian sculptor's work. The harmony of the lines encloses an emotional tension bordering on frenzy and the balance of the body is broken by the violence of its posture, for it is not being held up by the arms nor is it resting on its feet. The attitude is clearly untenable and suggests movement in the figure. Berruguete's habitual faults of technique are obvious only in the arms, which are disproportionately small, but this is a slight defect in comparison with the plastic perfection of the whole statue.

The head is small with delicate features and the golden hair is swept forward. Its look of intense pain is that of an unconsolable child, rather than that of a man, and is in keeping with the youthfulness of the body. As always, the whole figure is filled with emotion, even in the attitude of each limb, and in no other work did Berruguete obtain the same feeling of rending pain, both physical and mental, without lapsing into facile pathos. The anguished instability of the body's posture with the feet slipping up the tree-trunk is in itself enough to fill the spectator with a sense of painful anxiety even while he admires the beauty of the statue.

As usual, colour plays a very important part in the work. The flesh tints are amber and pink, and the draperies are gilt with dark blue painted borders. Although the body displays wounds, there are no arrows or even signs of bleeding.

The altar of San Benito was taken down and dismantled when the monastery was dissolved. After being stored in different places, various damaged pieces were exhibited in Santa Cruz Museum before being removed to the National Museum of Sculpture in Valladolid. There they have been carefully installed in a place of honour and re-grouped according to the original plan.

22. BERRUGUETE: SACRIFICE OF ISAAC. FROM THE ALTAR OF SAN BENITO.

Very few of Berruguete's figures for the altar of San Benito can be identified by their attributes. The only personages from the Old Testament that are recognizable are Moses, and Abraham sacrificing his son.

The *Sacrifice of Isaac* is one of the best known and most admired statues in the altar. Abraham is shown forcing his son to his knees on the altar with his hands behind his back; he grasps Isaac's hair with his left hand and is about to cut his throat with the other, after one last despairing glance at the heavens. His tense, rigid posture forms a contrast with that of his son, whose curving attitude is strikingly reminiscent of one of Michelangelo's youths in the vault of the Sistine Chapel.

As we have noticed, Berruguete's sculptures have a pictorial quality, for they were designed to be seen from only one vantage point. This is quite clear in the *Sacrifice of Isaac* and nearly all the other figures in the San Benito altarpiece. Berruguete could never have known that one day they would be seen in the round, for they were all made to be fitted into their respective niches where they could only be seen from the front, as with Donatello's statues for the Or San Michele and the *campanile* of the cathedral at Florence. It was

thus, with the figure of Isaac in profile, that Berruguete's composition had to be seen, for the plastic values to be fully appreciated.

The carving of Abraham is characteristically harsh and vigorous, but Isaac is modelled with unusual delicacy. Pieces of plastered fabric have been added to the draperies and the flesh parts have been painted. The colours are gilt covered by stippled patterns and simple decorative motifs for the borders. Berruguete uses characteristic bluish-black for the draperies, pale pink for Abraham's body, and rose-pink for Isaac's.

Berruguete's violent and dramatic temperament is seen at its most intense in this small work. The *Sacrifice of Isaac* was conceived in a grand manner, and even the traces of Michelangelo's influence fail to detract from its powerful originality and the emotional intensity of the contrasting figures of Abraham crying out in his torment, and the terrified Isaac.

23. BERRUGUETE: THE BRAZEN SERPENT. FROM THE CHOIR-STALLS IN TOLEDO CATHEDRAL.

Although the altar at San Benito cemented Berruguete's fame, his outstanding achievement was his carving for the choir-stalls in Toledo Cathedral. The lower portions of the stalls had been completed by the end of the fifteenth century, and the upper part was planned by Siloe and Covarrubias before 1529, when the contract for carving it was given to Vigarny and Berruguete who divided the work between them. Berruguete took the Epistles side, carving the reliefs on the back-rests and the alabaster figures above the *guardapolvos*. He also carved the colossal alabaster *Transfiguration* at the end of the choir and three small reliefs for the niche over the archbishop's stall which was the only one to be polychromed.

Berruguete had to enlist the help of expert artisans to complete his lively and original figures for the walnut panels of the stalls. But he gave free rein to his creative fancies in his three reliefs in the archbishop's throne which are almost concealed from view. They are carved with his usual careless technique and are full of a furious sense of movement, and a richness of composition which was unusual for him.

The two side reliefs in the niche are only 19½ inches in diameter and represent the *Crossing of the*

Red Sea and the *Brazen Serpent,* the latter being the one illustrated. The theme is taken from the Book of Exodus, in which the Hebrews are attacked by poisonous snakes on their journey through the wilderness and are cured by the sight of the Brazen Serpent set up by Moses. The subject provided Berruguete with a good excuse to create a balanced composition, full of feeling and movement. Once more he revealed his highly personal way of interpreting the Renaissance spirit in the way that his nudes are free from any hint of sensuality and delight in beauty for its own sake. His tortured, frenzied bodies have great expressive vitality, and the composition is far from confused, having both rhythm and even a certain symmetry. He used his habitual colours for the polychromy: a pale pink for the flesh parts, and dark blue on a sky-blue base for the draperies, with added touches of gold paint.

the shape of the bark and give the whole composition a circular quality. There is nothing disordered about their violent gestures, which harmonize with the fluid rhythm of the lines and different planes of the relief, which is graduated in depth towards the edges of the panel. The work would appear to have been done in a sudden burst of inspiration but also shows careful thought rather than hurried improvisation.

What is certain is that Berruguete reserved the carving of the three reliefs in the niche entirely for himself, and, while his skilful colleagues completed his figures for the choir-stalls, he allowed his talent full play in a spot where no one could make any alterations. His series of figures for the panels in the stalls and the *guardapolvos* are justly famed, but the genius and personality of this great and eccentric artist are revealed at their most intimate in these three small reliefs.

24. BERRUGUETE: THE LAST JUDGEMENT. FROM THE CHOIR-STALLS IN TOLEDO CATHEDRAL.

This is the central relief of the three decorating the niche for the archbishop's choir-stall and measures 33 inches in diameter. It is an extremely free rendering of the Last Judgement and is as untouched by Michelangelo's influence as it is by medieval tradition.

The scene has neither angels with their trumpets, demons, gaping tombs nor even the pit of hell itself. While the souls of the Blessed arise out of the blue waves towards heaven, the Damned huddle together in what might be Charon's boat in classical mythology. Christ is shown in the clouds above conversing with the Virgin who appears to be interceding on behalf of humanity.

There is nothing static or balanced in the composition which has all of Berruguete's typical restlessness. Instead of rising out of the ground, his figures come straight out of the turbulent sea. The accentuated curve of the bark suggests a state of constant oscillation on the waves, and Christ and his Mother seem to be perched rather insecurely on their cloud. Although the Blessed souls are more beautifully carved and carefully grouped, they are outnumbered by the Damned, but we have no means of knowing whether this was deliberately intended by the artist. The Damned are certainly the most interesting figures in the relief. The curves of their naked bodies emphasize

25 and 26. RECUMBENT EFFIGY OF DOÑA MENCÍA DE MENDOZA. CHAPEL OF THE CONSTABLE, BURGOS CATHEDRAL.

The Chapel of the Constable was founded in 1482 by the Constable of Castile, Don Pedro Hernández de Velasco and his wife. Their son Don Bernardino de Velasco commissioned Felipe Vigarny to make their tomb in 1527, and it is to this artist that the existing work has long been attributed.

This attribution has since been challenged by the discovery of a document stating that a certain Juan de Lugano had come from Genoa in 1557 with a consignment of Carrara marble intended for the tombs of Cardinal Tavera and the Constable and his wife. The various pieces of marble, which had all been roughly hewn after wax models made by Berruguete, included two statues, two pillows and four escutcheons for the Constable's tomb which were examined by experts and then declared to be similar to the artist's models. As Vigarny can obviously no longer be credited with the work, the evidence points to Berruguete as having received the commission at about the time the marble was brought over from Italy, and indeed before he died in 1561 he asked for payment to be made to his son, who is said to have undertaken most of the work.

In our opinion Berruguete did not even begin the work, for it shows no trace of his style either in the beautiful carving with its wealth of detail or in the

44

composition of the peaceful, robust figures which conform to the fashions of the time for funerary art. In order to lighten the load, they had been brought already roughly hewn from Italy, and could have been completed by some other artist after Berruguete's death in a free interpretation of the latter's models.

There is no evidence to show that Juan de Lugano was the sculptor, for all we know of him was that he worked in the Alcázar at Seville for an unspecified commission. All we can do is to point out the similarity between these effigies and others in the same Cathedral and the monastery at Oña which were carved by an unidentified artist who must have been a Castilian, judging by his style, and who carved grotesque figures in a style reminiscent of Siloe. What can definitely be asserted is that the talented Berruguete can never have had a hand in the effigies as we now see them.

Doña Mencía de Mendoza was the daughter of the great Castilian poet, the Marqués de Santillana. She had supervised the founding of the chapel while her husband the Constable was fighting at the siege of Granada, where he died in the year of the city's surrender. Doña Mencía survived him by eight years and died at the age of seventy-nine. The artist who carved her effigy made no attempt at portraiture and shows her as a mature woman with an impassive face showing traces of youth. She seems asleep rather than dead, with a faint smile playing about her lips, and she holds a rosary in her hands while a little lap-dog lies in the folds of her draperies. Every detail of her clothes, jewels and head-dress is carved with the utmost skill.

27. NICOLÁS DE VERGARA THE ELDER: DAVID DANCING BEFORE THE ARK OF THE COVENANT. RELIEF ON THE LECTERN IN TOLEDO CATHEDRAL (DETAIL).

The choir of Toledo Cathedral contains two magnificent iron lecterns decorated with reliefs in gilt bronze. They were made under Nicolás de Vergara's supervision by his son of the same name, and the goldsmith Juan Corbella. The models had been made under Vergara's direction by Juan Navarro in 1562, but the lecterns were only completed eight years later.

Nicolás de Vergara was the son of a Burgolese stone-cutter and the grandson of a Flemish glass-blower who had settled in Burgos. He had practised his grandfather's profession in Toledo ever since 1542, but he also worked in bronze, directing the work for the lecterns and the magnificent railings around Cardinal Cisneros's tomb at Alcalá de Henares which are no longer in existence. Although we do not know the extent to which Vergara worked in metal, the fact that he supervised the making of the lecterns seems to indicate that he planned the designs, including that of the reliefs. The lecterns stand on iron supports with Doric columns and entablatures and the gilt bronze reliefs decorate the reverse side of the book-rest. There are two rectangular reliefs on each lectern, representing biblical scenes. The detail illustrated comes from the lectern on the evangelist side of the choir and shows the removal of the Ark of the Covenant with David holding a harp and dancing among a group of young Hebrews.

Vergara's style illustrates the penetration of Spanish art by Italian Mannerism: the composition shows careful planning and thought and the technique is very correct, resulting from a thorough knowledge of the rules of drawing, perspective and composition, besides a mastery of relief carving. It is a mature work, free from any anxiety or problems, and an example of Renaissance art at its height before its inevitable decline.

28-32. JUAN DE JUNÍ: BURIAL OF CHRIST. NATIONAL MUSEUM OF SCULPTURE, VALLADOLID.

In Berruguete's opinion Juan de Juní was "the best foreign carver to come to Castile". He was probably born in the village of Joigny in Champagne about 1507, and nothing is known of his artistic training before he came to Spain. He suddenly made his appearance in 1532 together with some other French artists and at the beginning had no fixed workshop, settling wherever he obtained commissions. He came to Valladolid in 1541 after working in León, Salamanca and Medina de Rioseco. His first known work in this city was his *Burial of Christ* for the convent of San Francisco after a delay of five years.

This group of statues is one of Juní's greatest works and originally stood in the chapel founded by Fr. Antonio de Guevara, Bishop of Mondoñedo, the famous writer and preacher. It was carved between 1546 and 1548. The chapel was decorated with polychrome terracotta figures made by Jerónimo Corral, and with Juní's *Burial of Christ* on its altar it must have been a splendid sight, rivalling the other chapel of the Benavente family at Medina de Rioseco where the same artists worked and which is fortunately still in existence. The *Burial of Christ* was placed in a shell-niche between pairs of columns flanked by plaster figures of soldiers, as in Juní's later *Pietà* for Segovia Cathedral.

The Convent of San Francisco was destroyed during the secularization of the monasteries in 1837 and Juní's statues ended up in the museum, unfortunately without their original setting. No longer framed by their altarpiece they stand too close to the spectator and perhaps suffer from being over-lit. As a result it is certainly easier to study the statues in detail but they are all larger than life and seem to lack proportion among themselves. The figures were probably grouped more compactly in their original setting, as was customary in Juní's group sculptures, and their present position was determined by a desire to let the spectator appreciate each statue individually. Juní attached great importance to the grouping of his statues and their relationship to the structure of the altarpiece so that his other groups at Medina del Rioseco and Segovia have the advantage of being seen in their original settings.

The Valladolid *Burial of Christ* comprises seven figures which are carved entirely in the round except for the Virgin and St John, whose feet, like those of St Joseph and St Nicodemus cannot be seen, since the lower part of their bodies is hidden by the Dead Christ on his bier. The polychromy was always important in Juní's works and consists of pale burnished tints for the flesh parts and warm, rich colours for the *estofado* of the draperies.

When he made this work Juní had already spent thirteen years in Spain and had toned down the earlier violence that marked his style, modelling more delicately and giving his work a greater intensity of feeling. He was always a man of the north, with a Flemish rather than a French sensibility and a strong streak of sensuality that reminds one of Rubens. His statues express an impassioned sorrow in their gestures rather than in their faces: their emotion seems to come straight out towards the spectator, drawing him into the scene as a participant.

In the way they are now placed, the statues of the Virgin and St John are lower than the others and seem to be kneeling. They are, however, carved full length; the Virgin's inclined body shows that she is, in fact, on her knees. The violence of her grief is quite openly displayed instead of being confined and quietly repressed. Her emotion is emphasized by the way in which St John holds her in his arms as if to prevent her from flinging herself across the body of her Son.

Juní's work is steeped in a tragic sense of drama and is particularly suited to the expression of sorrow and suffering. Whenever the element of drama is lacking in any of his themes, his figures tend to gesticulate aimlessly in rhetorical mannerist attitudes. His figure of the Dead Christ has an almost classically modelled body and the exaggeratedly Baroque carving of the head lacks feeling, whereas the Virgin and the St John are deeply moving in their passionate sincerity and violent fervour.

The statue of the Magdalene is an example of how Juní's technical mastery attained an aesthetic value of its own. There is none of the improvisation that characterizes the work of Berruguete who used to work at full speed before the fires of his inspiration had time to die down. Juní carefully studied every detail as much for its own sake as for its relationship with the whole work. The right arm of the statue is bent, with its hand hidden in the folds of her draperies, while in her left hand she holds up a bottle of unguent with a elegantly affected gesture. The shape of her body is both hidden and revealed by the flowing draperies with their wealth of carefully planned curves and there is not an inch of surface that has not been lovingly chiselled by the artist. Her sorrow is suggested rather by the inclination of her head over her right shoulder than by her gestures, and Juní seems to have taken an especial delight in the carving of her graceful curving headdress and in the modelling of her young skin which invites the spectator's touch.

By contrast, the statue of Maria Salome is of an old woman with wrinkled face and a sunken mouth that seems to be repressing a sob. She is looking at the crown of thorns held in a piece of cloth rather than at the body of Christ and she holds up another piece of cloth in her right hand with a gesture that is difficult to explain unless it be to cover the crown which she seems to be reproaching for having wounded the temples of the Saviour. Her face is the most sincerely grief-stricken of all the figures in the group.

Juní's work tends to have a certain theatrical quality, although it is always tempered by good taste. It comes out especially in what I take to be the statue of Joseph of Arimathea, since Nicodemus, who was a priest of the Sanhedrin and doctor of the law, is more likely to be the old man with a beard by the feet of Christ. Joseph is shown as a clean-shaven elderly man with a head-dress and an ugly although somewhat feminine face. He is shown half-kneeling by the head of Christ, looking towards the spectator with his hand held out as if to invite contemplation of the scene. His uncovered right arm is a superb piece of realistic carving; as in the Magdalene, the left arm is hidden in the folds of his mantle with only the thumb showing. His face is a marvellous example of the typical tactile quality that Juní gave to his carving which never left a single plane of wood unfinished.

33. JUAN DE JUNÍ: SAINT JOHN THE BAPTIST. NATIONAL MUSEUM OF SCULPTURE, VALLADOLID.

This is one of Juní's most decidedly Baroque statues, and is the companion piece to a statue of the Magdalene, carved in partnership with Alonso Berruguete's son Inocencio. The sculptures were commissioned in 1551 by Doña Francisca de Villafana for the church in the monastery of San Benito at Valladolid and are now in the National Museum of Sculpture.

Whenever Juní dealt with an undramatic theme he tended to give his figures an aimless Mannerist sweep of movement, which was one of the risks inherent in his violent approach to his art. His earlier statue of the saint in Salamanca Cathedral was more elegant and restrained in its attitude, whereas the emotion in this work has been smothered in a swirling mass of curves and a complicated interplay of lines and surfaces. Technically it is a wonderful display of virtuosity, revealing a mastery of form and a boldness of composition, with the traditional lamb wrapped in the folds of the draperies. The saint's left hand is holding what might be part of a crucifix and his right hand points to the lamb but the gestures are somewhat affected. The opulent flesh parts give the figure a sleek rather than a muscled body, which is hardly in accordance with the usual ascetic image of the prophet, and the grief-stricken head is similarly unsuited to the theme.

Geniuses cannot always produce masterpieces and the only emotion that Juní succeeds in arousing with this statue is one of admiration for his skill in its composition and his masterly technique. Greater practice in the slower and more difficult process of stone-carving might have tempered his tendency towards superficial effects.

34. JUAN DE JUNÍ: RELIQUARY-BUST OF SAINT ANNE. NATIONAL MUSEUM OF SCULPTURE, VALLADOLID.

The history of this bust is unknown but it is certainly by Juní and one of his best works. It has strong affinities with some of the figures in the Valladolid *Pietà,* particularly the Magdalene and Maria Salome and both its carving and polychromy have been carried out with the greatest skill. It is a stupendously realistic work demonstrating Juní's characteristic and magnificent conception of form. The curves of the face, flabby and wrinkled with age, harmonize with the lines of the head-dress. The effect produced by the bust is heightened by the polychromy and warmly glowing gilt, which give it the sumptuous radiance of a metal reliquary. The very fact that it is only a bust figure precludes violent gestures and concentrates the spectator's attention on the features which are beautifully modelled and endowed with a sharply realistic expression.

35. GREGORIO FERNÁNDEZ: PIETÀ. CHURCH OF SAN MARTIN, VALLADOLID.

Although Gregorio Fernández was born in Galicia in about 1576, he can be regarded as a Castilian artist, having trained at Valladolid with Francisco de Rincón, Isaac de Juní and Leoni's colleagues and pupils. Although he turned to classical art for the study of proportions and composition, he was far from being a mannerist, and had a strange predilection for the art of the late Gothic period, as can be seen in the stiff, angular, broken lines of his figures draperies. The Renaissance taught him to appreciate the beauty of the human body and prevented him from giving way to the taste for unrestrained realism which marked the work of his followers. His statues are steeped in profound religious feeling and their great popularity made them into devotional images for the faithful.

This beautiful *Pietà* was carved for an altar in the convent of San Francisco which was destroyed in 1837; the sculptures were removed to the church of San Martín. The *Pietà* is not a processional image, for the back is cut flat in order that it fit into a niche. The work is not documented and its date is unknown, but it is certainly earlier than the famous *Pietà* in the National Museum of Sculpture.

Fernández's work shows a progressive simplification in carving technique and an increase of dramatic intensity. Of the two *Pietàs,* the *Dolorosa* of the San Martín version is the most serene and finely modelled, and on this basis we can place the date of the work between 1606, the first documented date in the artist's career, and 1616, when the second *Pietà* was made.

In its composition the group resembles Francisco de Rincón's work for the upper storey of the main altar in the Las Angustias church and this similarity helps to confirm the provisional dating of this piece, since one would expect Rincón's influence to show more strongly in Fernández's earlier work. The Virgin's similarity of posture with that of Juní's *Pietà* was almost certainly the result of direct influence.

When Fernández carved this *Pietà* he was already in full command of all his highly individual expressive resources. Less sensual than Juní in his modelling and more profound in his interpretation, Fernández approached his subject with the greatest sincerity. He never forgot that he was depicting the sorrow of a woman who was the Mother of God, which saved him from the temptation to humanize her figure too much. This *Dolorosa* is undoubtedly his most beautiful. The pathos of her attitude with uplifted hands distracts one's attention to some slight extent from the grief in her face. The composition was designed to fit easily into its niche in the altarpiece and Christ's body is almost entirely reclining in his Mother's lap. The delicate modelling of the flesh parts resembles that of the *Dead Christ* of El Pardo as does the carving of the hair, shown falling in long humid locks over the shoulders. The beauty of the sculpture is strikingly enhanced by the polychromy even though it was somewhat restored when the work was removed to its present location.

36 and 37. GREGORIO FERNÁNDEZ: PIETÀ. NATIONAL MUSEUM OF SCULPTURE, VALLADOLID.

In 1616 the penitential church of Las Angustias, Valladolid, commissioned Fernández to carve a new *Pietà* as a *paso* or processional figure. It was placed in the transept chapel on the Evangelist side of the church, facing Juan de Juní's statue of the *Virgen de los Cuchillos* (Virgin of the Swords) which itself was accompanied by statues of *St John* and the *Magdalene,* also by Fernández. They may originally have been placed with the *Pietà* together with the statues of the two thieves as they now are in the Museum.

Fernández did not carve many figures for *pasos* and the greater part of those attributed to his hand were produced by his workshop almost entirely independently of his direction. Fernández was thirty-eight years old when he was given the contract for this *Pietà* and was at the height of his artistic powers. As the figures were to be carried in religious processions they were carved in the round so that they could be admired from every vantage point. Christ is shown with His head and shoulders in His Mother's lap, as in the San Martín *Pietà*, but this time His legs are fully extended on the ground instead of being bent. The Virgin supports the body with her left hand while the right is outstretched. She is gazing up at the sky as though to implore help in her sorrow, in a peculiarly eloquent and dramatic attitude. The contrast between the pathos of her grief-stricken countenance and that of Christ, serene in death, is much stronger than in the San Martín *Pietà*.

The carving is very restrained. There is nothing exaggeratedly realistic in the treatment of Christ's head and body and the Virgin's face and hands. Christ's body has similarities with others by Fernández, such as the first of its kind at El Pardo, but it is more peaceful and restrained in its pose and has a special beauty of its own. The rather schematic carving of the draperies emphasizes Fernández's habitual angular, broken lines.

We know from the contract that the polychromy was by the painter Marcelo Martínez, and we also have dates for the re-painting of the *Pietà* in the eighteenth century, which is apparent in its present state. The colours are spoilt by being too matt and harsh: the flesh-tints are a grey-white and clash with the discordant tones of the draperies. These faults cannot be attributed to Martínez, since we know that Fernández, who was not a painter, always took great care in choosing his collaborators for fear that inferior polychromy would spoil his carving.

The theme of the work, the Dead Christ lying in the Virgin's lap, was known as "The Fifth Sorrow" and was a late Gothic theme, afterwards spreading throughout Flemish and German painting and sculpture. A great number of small Flemish figures of this type are found in Spain with compositions closely resembling that of Fernández's work. That they may have directly influenced him would explain not only the similarity of attitudes, but also his Gothic treatment of draperies in stiff angular lines that are so very different from the smoothly flowing and restrained style encouraged by the Renaissance.

38 and 39. GREGORIO FERNÁNDEZ: DEAD CHRIST. NATIONAL MUSEUM OF SCULPTURE, VALLADOLID.

Like all great artists Fernández created certain types which were to survive in the work of his pupils and imitators. One of the most diffused was that of the recumbent *Dead Christ*, for which the prototype was made for King Philip III, who later gave it to the Capuchin Church of El Pardo. Ever since the eighteenth century the traditional date given for the Pardo *Christ* was 1605, which is surprisingly early in view of its mature style, and we now know that it could not have been carved before 1614. The work shows the Dead Christ laid out on an altar cloth with His head propped up on a cushion, and it proved so popular that it was followed by a number of similar versions from Fernández's workshop, some by his own hand and others copied by his imitators. Worth mentioning are the *Dead Christs* in the San Plácido and Encarnación convents in Madrid, in the Museum and churches of Santa Ana, Sancti-Spiritus and Santa Catalina in Valladolid, and those in the cathedrals at Segovia, Zamora and Medina del Pomar, among others. Of all the figures those at San Plácido and El Sacramento most closely resemble the Pardo *Christ*.

The *Dead Christ* here illustrated was carved for the Madrid headquarters of the Jesuits which was later converted into the Oratory of San Felipe Neri.

When the church was destroyed the statue was removed to the former church of Buen Suceso and when that too disappeared, the *Christ* went into the Prado Museum, which finally gave it to the Museum at Valladolid when it became the National Museum of Sculpture. It is still there today, and is known as the *Christ of the Filipini* or *Christ of Good Fortune* (Buen Suceso).

The modelling of the flesh parts is drier and more restrained than in the Pardo *Christ*, showing the artist's tendency towards simplification during his middle period. The stiff lines of the draperies are emphasized, as is the straightness of the shoulders, which may have been intentional since the work is always viewed laterally. On the other hand the head is impressive and full of pathos, being slightly raised in the Pardo statue and not falling forward over the chest as in the *Dead Christ* in San Plácido. The curling hair falls in damp-looking strands over the forehead and the pillow—one of Fernández's characteristic touches—and the curling beard is forked. The dramatic expression of the features is emphasized by the down-turned eyes and half-open mouth and in its inspired realism has a nobility and grace worthy of the subject.

Unfortunately the image was re-painted, probably in the eighteenth century, with harsh matt tints for the flesh parts and exaggerated black and white for the draperies. The cushion no longer has the original polychromy, which imitated the texture of embroideries and which can be seen in Fernández's other figures which have not been retouched. The bad polychromy might explain why the modelling of this work appears to be inferior to that of the figures in Madrid which have remained completely intact in their original form.

40-44. GREGORIO FERNÁNDEZ: BAPTISM OF CHRIST. NATIONAL MUSEUM OF SCULPTURE, VALLADOLID.

This great relief formed the central portion of the altar in the chapel of St John in the monastery of the Barefooted Carmelites at Valladolid. Don Antonio de Camporredondo, a judge in the supreme Council became patron of the chapel in 1623. The following year he commissioned an altar for it, giving the commission for the sculpture to Fernández. When the convent was destroyed both the church and the

49

chapel survived, but the main relief was removed to the museum.

It is a very large work with life-size figures carved in the round rather than in relief and attached to their background. Fernández did very little relief carving and contented himself with placing his figures against a panel without receding planes, but in some reliefs he did carve a few simple architectural perspectives. He had already treated the same theme in one of his reliefs for the altar of the two SS John at Nava del Rey, but this was smaller and rather carelessly carved in comparison with this later work which deserves to be called a masterpiece.

The simplicity of the composition is characteristic of Fernández. The statues of Christ and the Baptist occupy most of the area of the panel, the upper part only having a few cherubs' heads and small clouds with a diminutive figure of the Heavenly Father to give a sense of perspective to the relief. The background with a river and mountains is merely suggested and is painted on the wood.

St John is wearing a camel-hair tunic and a cloak; his chest is bared, and he is holding up a shell with which to baptise Christ kneeling on the rocks. The figure of Christ is more amply covered than in the Nava del Rey version, though His legs and shoulders are bare. St John seems somewhat afraid and disconcerted by the Messiah's humility, for his muscles are contracted as if to withhold his gesture of baptism.

The work is perfect in every respect. St John's bare torso is a masterly piece of carving and much more studied and realistic than was usual in Fernández's sculpture. The long disordered strands of his hair frame a tense face with stiffened muscles and half open mouth. The way he holds his cloak in his left hand is both elegant and natural. In contrast to the saint's impassioned attitude, Christ has an air of solitude and resignation and His face is serene. The statue has close affinities with Fernández's *Dead Christs* and *Crucifixions,* which would suggest that the artist's ideal conception of the Holy Face was the same for all his representations.

The original polychromy has survived in very good condition. The flesh tints are a light matt for Christ and a burnished tone for the Baptist, as befits a man living in the open. St John's tunic is blue and his cloak dark red; Christ's draperies are a bluish grey. The subject is rounded off with light colours for the clouds, the Holy Ghost and God the Father, but they add nothing to the aesthetic value of the composition.

45. GREGORIO FERNÁNDEZ: SAINT TERESA. NATIONAL MUSEUM OF SCULPTURE, VALLADOLID.

St Teresa, the great saint of Castile, was a favourite subject in seventeenth-century Spanish art, after her canonization. The statue that Fernández made on commission for the Carmelite Convent in Valladolid in 1624 served as a prototype and was afterwards copied by all Castilian sculptors. The prior of the convent, Padre Orbea, was a good friend and patron to Fernández, giving him numerous commissions for carvings in various other convents of the same order. Fernández lived near Padre Orbea's convent and when he died in 1636 he was buried in its chapel. His statues for the convent included a Carmelite *Virgin,* now lost, which was reputed to be one of his finest works, and the central relief for the main altar, together with his *Santa Magdalena de Pazis* and *St Teresa,* now all acquired by the museum.

The statue illustrated is one of the artist's later works and is very simply modelled. The draperies fall in straight, rigid folds with the front of the mantle projecting forward away from the body. The saint holds a book in her left and a pen in her raised right hand as if awaiting divine inspiration. The head, revealing something of her inner fervour, is correctly but coldly modelled with upturned eyes and a slightly opened mouth. There is none of the thrilling sense of reality that animates Fernández's other statues.

The statue was certainly a success and served as a model for all later representations. Fernández himself copied it the following year for the Carmelites at Medina de Rioseco with much greater intensity of expression in its ecstatic face and more meticulous carving enhanced by rich polychromy with foliage patterns painted on the draperies, but the Valladolid *St Teresa* seems to have been repainted in the eighteenth century.

46 and 47. JUAN MARTÍNEZ MONTAÑÉS: SAINT JEROME. ALTAR OF SAN ISIDORO DEL CAMPO, SEVILLE.

Juan Martínez Montañés was nick-named the "God of Wood-carving" by his contemporaries and enjoyed in his own lifetime a fame which has neither faded nor been eclipsed three and a half centuries later. Not only was he always regarded by the ordinary people as a religious sculptor of genius, also but erudite opinion has not dared disparage him, even when it has been most hostile to Spanish polychrome sculpture as a whole. The reason is that Montañés's obvious mastery of his art, his aesthetic feeling, and his almost classical sense of composition have put him beyond the range of hostile criticism and proved him to be one of the very great sculptors of all time.

Montañés was born in 1568 and, like Fernández, trained during the sixteenth century but only showed his full artistic personality in the seventeenth century; his few known works dating from before 1603 show little difference from the styles then prevalent in Seville.

Although he was born in Alcalá la Real, he had first trained at Granada together with Pablo de Rojas and had already settled in Seville at the age of eighteen, remaining there for the rest of his very long life, until his death in 1649. He was not a precocious artist and his greatest creative period dates from 1603, when he carved the *Christ of Clemency,* to 1620, the probable date of his *Christ of the Passion,* after which he was content to direct the productions of his workshop, intervening directly in only a few works.

The main altar at the church of the monastery of St Jerome in Santiponce, near Seville, is deservedly one of his most famous works. It was carved when he was at the height of his powers as a sculptor between 1609 and 1613, and he designed its structure himself. Although the figure sculpture was done in his workshop the most important work was by his own hand, especially his highly original *St Jerome,* which, according to the letter of the contract, had to be entirely his own work and "without any outside help".

That Torrigiani's statue of *St Jerome* influenced Sevillian sculptors would explain Montañés's own version, in which he had tried to emulate the former's masterly technique. It is quite certain that Montañés himself — not the most modest of men — realized to what extent he had surpassed the Florentine's very academic work. Whereas the modelling of Torrigiani's *St Jerome* is idealized, almost irritating in its perfection, Montañés's version was inspired by his direct observation of reality.

Montañés's interpretation of the saint was not traditional, for, instead of being an old man ravaged by penance, his *St Jerome* is a mature man with a lean but robust build. Pacheco, who, as in so many other of Montañés's statues, painted the flesh parts, pointed out that the saint was only thirty years old when he did penance in the Syrian desert. However,

in view of the prevailing conventions, it would have been too daring an iconographic innovation to have depicted him as such a young man. Despite this and perhaps because of Pacheco's influence, Montañés's *St Jerome* is less aged than in an earlier version he made for his altar at Santa Clara, Llerena, which was finished in 1604. This direct ancestor of the Santiponce statue seems to have been inspired not only by Torrigiani, but even more by one of his followers, Jerónimo Hernández, whose *St Jerome* for a relief in Seville Cathedral has a greater degree of realism and expression.

Like Torrigiani and Hernández, Montañés also showed his earlier *St Jerome* with the arm extended holding a stone as if he were about to strike himself on the chest, but he differed in making his figure kneel —an attitude he repeated in his second version. The carving of the flesh parts shows his advance towards naturalistic treatment, but the style of the head is that of a previous generation of sculptors, having affinities with the work of Ocampo and Núñez Delgado.

In the later statue for the church of San Isidoro del Campo, Montañés showed progress not only in his splendid handling of flesh parts but also in his whole approach to sculpture. The saint's arm is bent against his chest as though striking it and the gesture gives the whole composition a more unified silhouette. The crucifix is held nearer the severe and restrained face of the saint, which has an expression of spiritual yearning towards Christ rather than one of drama. The statue was carved in the round so that it might be carried in religious processions and is seen against a low-relief background of landscape with a tree and a lion stretched out on a rock.

Pacheco used his skill to the utmost in the painting of this statue, as in Montañés's *St Dominic*, and in his treatise on painting even cited his technique for the work as an example of how flesh parts should be painted. The result of such close collaboration between painter and sculptor was to be one of the finest pieces of realistic sculpture ever created in Spain.

48-54. MONTAÑÉS: THE NATIVITY. ALTAR OF SAN ISIDORO DEL CAMPO, SEVILLE.

The altar of San Isidoro del Campo at Santiponce near Seville consists of a central panel with compartments for the figure of *St Jerome* in the lower story, *St Isidore* above in the centre, an *Assumption* above, and two large reliefs in each of the wings, with scenes of the *Nativity,* the *Adoration of the Kings,* the *Resurrection,* and the *Ascension.* The altar is flanked by effigies of the two *St Johns* standing outside and somewhat below the main structure, and is crowned by a *Calvary* and four *Virtues.* Montañés's direct intervention in the altar was confined to the lower storeys, and, with his figures, his two reliefs are the finest works in the whole piece.

The *Nativity* would appear to be wholly by Montañés's own hand, as much by its composition as by its masterly carving which reveals a profound knowledge of relief technique. It comprises a series of receding planes with figures carved almost in the round standing against a background which is completed with a glimpse of distant landscape painted over the wood. The composition is centred around the Infant Christ lying in a basket-cradle surrounded by a semi-circular group comprising the figures of the kneeling Virgin, St Joseph and a shepherd. The upper part of the relief, above St Joseph's head, is bisected by the vertical line of the stable wall, with another shepherd and the looming heads of two cows on the right, and two reverently inclined angels on the left. The whole scene has a serene and contemplative quality, and a kind of classical simplicity, entirely free from any artistic or sentimental straining after effect.

Although Montañés was a realist he shrank from depicting the Infant Christ as a new-born baby, as did the Flemish primitives, and followed the Italian convention by representing a well-developed child. The Infant's nudity and the way the Virgin holds the draperies, as though she has just unwrapped Him for the benefit of the shepherds, may also be due to Italian influence. The execution of the heads is extremely fine: the contemplative Virgin has a delicate oval-shaped face, and St Joseph bears a great resemblance to Montañés's representations of Christ and is unmistakably a young man. This was a convention in Andalusian art, which always gave St Joseph a greater importance in compositions of this kind than did Flemish or even Italian art. A touch of popular realism is given to the scene by the two shepherds with their frankly anachronistic costumes; lastly, the two angels representing celestial homage to the Child are among Montañés's very finest creations and by their perfection and elegance might have been carved by Donatello himself.

In this, as in all his works, Montañés shows the care he took to interpret his themes with the greatest propriety, concentrating on the religious and theological rather than the historical aspects. Instead of making his themes the pretext for a display of artistic virtuosity he approached them with the respect and pious reverence of one who seeks to serve his ideals by his art. It is this that explains his success as a religious sculptor: not only is the spectator enchanted by the beauty of the relief but the believer is stirred by the mystery of the Son of God, as it is revealed.

55. MONTAÑÉS: SAINT JOHN THE BAPTIST. ALTAR OF SAN ISIDORO DEL CAMPO, SEVILLE.

The relief of the *Nativity* is an illustration of how Montañés used his art to compose and interpret a theme. The statues of the two St Johns show us how he carved figures in the round.

The statue of St John the Baptist is slightly less than life-size and has a classical posture, standing with the right foot forward and elegantly swathed in a cloak which reveals the traditional hair tunic underneath. Montañés has not stressed the saint's ascetic aspect: instead of being the 'voice crying in the wilderness', he is shown lost in contemplation of the Lamb, reclining on his book, and pondering the mystery of Christ. His expression is that of a man wrapped up in his thoughts. The features are clear-cut, even lively, with sunken cheeks and lofty brow and the length of his face is accentuated by a smooth beard and long flowing hair, falling over his forehead in short locks.

Whatever carving in this figure is due to Montañés's workshop assistants, the head is certainly his own work. The delicacy of its modelling and its intensity of expression could only come from his hand, and it is this that distinguishes all his carvings from those of his pupils: a difference which is hard to put into words but which is immediately striking. It is as if Montañés could give soul to the very wood by his carving.

56 and 57. MONTAÑÉS: THE IMMACULATE CONCEPTION. SEVILLE CATHEDRAL.

The representation of the Virgin meditating on the mystery of her Immaculate Conception is a late theme in Christian iconography and was certainly unknown before the fifteenth century. At first it was linked with the Assumption, the Virgin being shown with the moon and angels at her feet. In the sixteenth century the theme became increasingly important until it finally overtook the traditional representations of the Madonna with the Infant Christ in her arms. A contributing factor for its popularity in the seventeenth century was the famous discovery at Sacro Monte, Granada, in 1595 of the "leaden books" which contained in Arabic the phrase "Mary was not tainted by original sin." The ensuing theological controversy dragged on until 1682, when the statement was definitely ascertained as apocryphal. Despite the verdict, the impassioned arguments that had resulted from the discovery gave rise to an outburst of Marian worship which was crystallised in the image of the "Immaculate and pure Conception." The driving force behind this Marian enthusiasm was Don Pedro de Castro, Archbishop of Granada and later of Seville, which explains the popularity enjoyed by images of the *Immaculate Conception* in both cities, so great that it later earned for Andalusia the name of "Land of the Blessed Virgin" *(Tierra de María Santísima)*.

The prototype for this image is to be found in the altar of San Jerónimo in Granada and is almost certainly by Juan Bautista Vázquez, *el Mozo,* at the close of the sixteenth century. It inspired similar works by Pablo de Rojas who was Montañés's master, and this even before similar statues were being carved at Seville by Núñez Delgado and his pupil Ocampo, which did not differ essentially from those being made in Granada. They all show the Virgin in a long tunic and a cloak, with one end tucked up under her left arm. The head is nearly always uncovered with the hair flowing down over the shoulders, the eyes downcast, the hands together, and the feet resting on a crescent moon with the horns pointing downwards, accompanied by one or several cherubs' heads and, in some cases, by a serpent or dragon.

Montañés made his first *Immaculate Conception* for the church of El Pedroso in 1606. Its only difference from the models which inspired it lay in the greater impression of movement in the figure and in the fall of the draperies. His own interpretation of the theme was determined by his statue for the cathedral which is more delicately carved but not basically different from the prototype. With this work Montañés entered into his brilliant final period of artistic activity, for, although he was becoming an old man

he had lost none of his creative powers. The statue is still in its original site, in the altar or one of the chapels known as *Los Alabastros* on the south side of the choir, which had been given to Dona Jerónima de Zamudio as a tomb for herself and her husband, Francisco Gutiérrez de Molina. She commissioned Montañés for the altar in 1628, fixing the cost at 3,600 ducats.

The *Immaculate Conception* is somewhat less than life-size. The silhouette of the figure is broadened by the ample draperies which only give a hint of the body beneath and fall in large folds, with the forepart tucked under the left arm, lessening the overall impression of heaviness with their deep shadowed furrows. The frontal aspect of the statue is slightly modified by the way the head inclines towards the right, with the left foot pointing in the opposite direction. The bold *chiaroscuro* of the draperies is painted over an exquisitely gilded ground, and the head, with its purity of line and long hair flowing loosely over the shoulders on either side of the tawny face with its almost adolescent smoothness, is brought alive by a repressed smile, suggested only vaguely by the curve of the lips. The expression of purity is enhanced by the lowered eyes. The statue was given the popular nick-name of "The Little Blind One" *(La Cieguecita)* but whether this is because of its half-shut eyes or the Andalusian taste for hyperbole it is hard to say.

Montañés's *Virgin* is as divinely human as it is the essence of virginal feminity. She represents an exaltation of womanhood at its most pure and perfect and is free from the slightest hint of sensuality. The three faultlessly carved cherub's heads and the crescent moon at her feet confirm that the theme could be none other than the *Immaculate Conception.* The altarpiece in which it is placed was carved wholly by Montañés's own hand and is decorated with paintings by Pacheco, two small images of St John the Baptist and St Gregory, and various reliefs with busts of SS Joseph, Joaquin, Jerome and Francis.

58. MONTAÑÉS: SAINT DOMINIC. MUSEUM OF FINE ARTS, SEVILLE.

Montañés made his first important altarpiece in 1605 for the convent of Santo Domingo de Portacoeli outside the walls of Seville in the San Bernardo quarter. Neither the convent nor the altar are any longer in existence, and of the eight reliefs in the latter the only two that were known to have survived were burnt in the church of San Bernardo in 1936. Only the titular image of the saint was saved, being removed from the altar during the Dissolution of the Monasteries, and it is now one of the prize exhibits of the museum. Although it was made for the main compartment in the altarpiece, it is finely carved entirely in the round and can be appreciated from any angle.

St Dominic is shown as a half-naked, kneeling penitent, holding a crucifix in his left hand and a scourge in the right. The statue is life-size and its beautiful polychromy adds to its realism. The carving of the flesh parts shows a careful study of anatomy and proves how far Montañés had moved away from the mannerist conventions of his predecessors. But, as in this statue, Montañés's realism was always tempered by his sense of proportion and beauty which saved it from excesses and gave dignity to all his sculpture. There is both nobility and naturalism in the statue's posture, in the modelling of the body and the treatment of the draperies. The carving of the head is very characteristic of Montañés and could not have been derived from his masters. It combines a classical perfection of features with an intensity of expression that seems to reveal the very soul of the saint.

The painting of this marvellous statue was carried out by Pacheco, according to his own statement. He reverted to sixteenth century technique by using burnish over a plaster preparation, and limited himself to one coat of glue and white-lead as a base before adding a matt oil paint as a priming. The rest of the process was the same as for oil painting, consisting of fine brush strokes and a smooth *chiaroscuro* to enhance the carving. Polychromy was no longer the mere addition of colour by a routine craftsman and had become the object of a close partnership between painter and sculptor. As a result the work was conceived in terms of colour as much as form, both guided by reality.

59. MONTAÑÉS: SAINT BRUNO. MUSEUM OF FINE ARTS, SEVILLE.

Montañés was already seventy years old when he carved this magnificent statue of *St Bruno* for the Charterhouse of Las Cuevas at Seville. It was made after the artist had gone through a largely barren and critical period of some years, before recovering his mastery and creating yet another series of masterpieces. By this time he had shed the last vestiges of the classicism that lingered so long in his work and had whole-heartedly embraced realism.

The theme of St Bruno brought good fortune to its interpreters. The saint was carved by nearly all the best Spanish sculptors of the seventeenth century, among them Pereyra, Gregorio Fernández, Montañés, and twice by José de Mora in the Charterhouse of Granada, and their statues were all famous. Every sculptor gave his own interpretation to the saint's personality: some showed him as an ascetic, others as a mystic, a man of action, or else of quiet contemplation. In Montañés's version the saint is ascetic rather than mystical and his magnificently realistic head shows no trace of the classical conventions that were so frequent a feature of the artist's work, even in his maturity. We are shown a man of action an organiser, gazing at his crucifix to receive the inspiration and strength necessary for him to impose the constitution of his order as set down in the book he is holding. His fine head with its shaven skull and lean features is tremendously realistic as are also the hands, a part of the body in which Montañés's carving always excels. Similarly his white habit is carved with sober naturalism.

If Baroque art is defined as a reaction to the classical style, and as the artistic expression of reality freed from all convention and aesthetic bias, then we must acknowledge Montañés as being a Baroque artist in his last phase. His sculpture, as in this figure, had become a way of creating life. His *St Bruno* is so real and profoundly human that like Pereyra's version at Miraflores, it seems almost to speak.

60. JUAN DE MESA: HEAD OF SAINT JOHN THE BAPTIST. SEVILLE CATHEDRAL.

This beautiful head comes from the Sevillian convent of Santa Clara where it was kept out of sight in the cloister until only a few years ago. It had been attributed to Montañés, but its style differs greatly from the head in his altar in the convent of San Leandro which has his characteristic classic touch and elegance. The Santa Clara head by contrast, has a Baroque feeling of form with its wavy hair piled up on the forehead into the typical cluster that was first used by Núñez Delgado and Montañés, and then exaggerated by Juan de Mesa. The latter's style is also apparent in the modelling of the features whose characteristic drama is heightened by the polychromy.

Despite the traditional attribution of this work to Montañés, and the more recent claims made for Núñez Delgado, Hernández Díaz has declared Mesa to have been the artist. His statement is backed up by a document dated 1625 which is a declaration by the silversmith Juan Vázquez Cano to the effect that he had been commissioned that same year to make a casket, a platter and a diadem for a head of St John which had been carved on the instructions of the Mother Superior of the Convent, Doña Isabel de Ribera.

The theme had already been anticipated in Sevillian art for Gaspar Núñez Delgado had made a similar head in terracotta: a magnificent piece of work signed by the artist and now in the González Nandín Collection at Seville. Montañés also had made a head of St John for the convent of San Leandro prior to Mesa's work. The theme was later repeated by Felipe de Ribas, probably after one of Cano's models, for the altar of Santa Paula, and it continued to be interpreted frequently in Spanish sculpture until the eighteenth century. Mesa's head is peculiar in that it seems to have been designed to be placed upright, judging by the carving of the hair which flows past the face. It is unlike either Núñez Delgado's head, which is placed with the mouth upwards and the hair falling back away from the head, or the two heads by Montañés and Ribas respectively, both of which lie on one side. Could the way the hair flows be due to the way the head originally placed? It if had been made to stand upright this could explain the disappearance of the original casket, tray and diadem, which were replaced by the existing base on which the head lies on its side.

61. JUAN DE MESA: VIRGEN DE LAS CUEVAS (VIRGIN OF THE GROTTO). MUSEUM OF FINE ARTS, SEVILLE.

Of all Montañés's pupils, the Cordoban Juan de Mesa is the most striking example of an artist who has only recently become famous after centuries of total obscurity, through having had his art too closely

identified with that of his master. It was only when documents came to light in the Sevillian archives that it was found that many of Montañés's most popular statues were in fact the work of his pupil, including the *Christ of Great Power* and most of the *Crucifixions* belonging to the Sevillian confraternities, not to mention the most beautiful of all at San Pedro, Vergara. In the same way, the statue of the Virgin for the charterhouse at Las Cuevas was held to be by the master, until documentary evidence pointed to Mesa.

Montañés had carved two small altars for the charterhouse and in 1621 was commissioned to make a *Virgin and Child* and a *St John the Baptist*. He was unable to fulfil the contract for some unknown reason and in 1623 the work went instead to Juan de Mesa. Both figures are among that part of his work that was most influenced by Montañés and they prove the extent to which the two styles had become fused. It is more than probable that Mesa actively collaborated with Montañés and that his death in 1627 contributed to the master's decline and failing powers in his period of crisis at that time.

Juan de Mesa was more dramatic and Baroque than Montañés, the difference in their styles being most apparent in the theme of the *Crucifixion*. On the other hand the *Virgin* of Las Cuevas remains faithful to Montañés's aesthetic, with its tranquil flow of lines and the way the figure is broadened towards the base by the fall of the draperies. The precedent for this figure was set by Montañés's statue for the small altar in the Oratory of San Isidoro del Campo, in which the attitude is similar, though the lines are more restful and the silhouette slimmer. In his own version Mesa emphasized the realistic character of his theme and accentuated the Baroque *chiaroscuro* of the folds of the draperies.

The image is less than life-size and is carved in cedar-wood as was customary for such special works. The original polychromy has survived and consists of clear tones and gold decorations on the draperies.

62 and 63. ALONSO CANO: SAINT JOHN THE BAPTIST. GÜELL COLLECTION, BARCELONA.

Alonso Cano was one of the most remarkable figures of the seventeenth century in Spain. A master of painting, sculpture and architecture, he was also an art-theorist, bibliophile, print-collector and indefatigable sketcher. A man of fascinating and often contradictory character, he exerted a great influence on his contemporaries and on the art of Seville, Granada and Madrid – the three cities where above all others he preferred to work. We now know that he studied painting with Velázquez under Pacheco, but not where he learned sculpture, which he considered the inferior of the two arts. He was obsessed by painting, and it was not until he gave it up, perhaps because of Zurbarán's rivalry, that he fully devoted himself to sculpture until his departure from Seville. The fact that he contracted no works in his own name until 1630, suggests that until then he had been working in his father's studio exposed to Montañés's influence, which was then dominant in Sevillian sculpture. A number of works can be attributed to Cano's early period, but although beginning to reveal a personal style, they are in all essentials inspired by Montañés.

The *St John* in the Güell Collection originally came from Seville and would seem to be the same statue that Cano carved in 1624 for the church of San Juan de la Palma. He also made an altar for the church which was removed in the nineteenth century to the village of San Juan de Aznalfarache, while the statue remained in Seville, but no longer in its church. When Cano began the *St John* he had already completed the main structure of an altar for the parish church of Lebrija, which was the first work contracted in his own name and showed his emancipation from Montañés's influence – a process that was to continue until Cano had evolved a radically different style of his own.

The saint is shown as a young man, almost an adolescent, as in Montañés's similar figure for the convent of San Leandro, but the posture is different, for Cano's *St John* is seated with the Lamb supported on one knee. This pose was later copied by Montañés himself for his two versions of the saint for the churches of Santa Paula and Santa Ana, carved late in his career after Cano had gone to Madrid. Although the statue is seated, his attitude is far from restful, for the body is tensed and full of movement, unlike Montañés's figures with their self-contained serenity of expression and classically handled draperies. The long, loosely flowing hair frames a face which is serious and full of deep thought for all its apparent youthfulness. The adolescent body is only half covered by the camel-hair tunic and is modelled with a correctness of line, but also a frank naturalism that owes nothing to Renaissance influence. The original polychromy has survived in a somewhat darkened state on the flesh parts, but the draperies have been repainted. The gilt can still be seen shining through the later coats of red in the *estofado* that was used by Cano in imitation of Montañés and which he later abandoned for a different technique.

Cano's Baroque style as shown in this work did not rely on violent theatrical gestures, swirling draperies and exuberant forms; it is rather to be seen in the way he evoked a feeling of restlessness that was sometimes mingled with sorrow and in his deliberate rejection of classical formulas.

64. ALONSO CANO: THE IMMACULATE CONCEPTION. GRANADA CATHEDRAL.

Cano did little sculpture while he was living at the court as the King's Painter, but when he went to Granada as prebendary to the cathedral he not only enriched it with his paintings for the main chapel and his design for the new façade, but also carved several statues, including a beautiful *Immaculate Conception* for the shrine above the great lectern in the choir which is also his work.

The statuette has been lovingly carved in cedarwood. Its very smallness adds to its charm for it only stands twenty inches high. Cano enjoyed making such small works, for he was able to complete them before his inspiration had given out and without any assistance, and, also, because he no longer had his own workshop after leaving Seville. When he carved the figure he did not consider the fact that if it were to be placed in its shrine above the lectern it would have been too high to have been properly seen by the spectator. He made full use of his talents and worked on the statuette as though he were chasing a fine piece of silver, taking the greatest pains with every detail and then painting it with all his skill. It was hardly surprising, therefore, that the cathedral authorities refused to let the figure go to its original destination. Instead, they placed it on a chest of drawers in the sacristy where it could be appreciated at close quarters, and there it has remained to this day. Cano then carved another statuette for the lectern, the *Virgin of Bethlehem,* which was a very elegant work but not as beautiful as the first.

Cano set a new pattern for his images of the Virgin by giving them a diamond-shaped silhouette, rather like that of an inverted pyramid. The first of this type which became highly characteristic of Cano's later style, was the statue for the altar at Lebrija. The draperies reached their widest extent at the centre and were then progressively tapered towards the feet which were hidden in the folds. The same style was repeated in his paintings at Madrid, and all the monuments of his last period at Granada, but it was most emphasized in his treatment of the theme of the *Immaculate Conception*. The tapering silhouette of the statuette in Granada Cathedral is so accentuated that the figure seems to be suspended above the ground, barely touching its base which is shaped like a cloud containing a crescent moon and four cherubs' heads. There is an absence of straight lines in the composition: the tunic and the mantle are full of twisting, curving folds, and their restless sense of movement forms a striking contrast to the serenity and pure lines of the face and hands. The hair flows smoothly over the back and shoulders, following the contours of the body so as not to disrupt the fluid beauty of its lines, and the hands are clasped slightly to one side, thus preventing the composition from appearing too severely symmetrical. The face is almost that of a child with its enormous almond-shaped eyes, finely shaped nose and diminutive mouth. The whole work is a perfect example of the ideal beauty that Cano sought to express in all his works – a beauty that transcended form to become a quality of the spirit. The Virgin's expression is one of quiet contemplation as if she is absorbed in the wonder and mystery of her destiny.

The beautiful polychromy has been executed with an oil-painting technique that Cano had learned from Pacheco. The colours are pale brown for the face, chestnut brown and black for the hair, a bluish-white for the tunic and blue for the mantle, the last being darkened by later repainting when varnish was used to give a sheen to the draperies. The cloud under the Virgin's feet is decorated with shades of gilt, following the traditional technique of *estofado*.

It would not be an exaggeration to say that the theme of the *Immaculate Conception* finds its most perfect plastic expression in this statuette. This is borne out by its success, for all Cano's pupils, especially Pedro de Mena, made copies and imitations that have survived to this day. But no one could repeat the almost ethereal elegance of Cano's work and, as time went on, their versions deteriorated in quality.

65. ALONSO CANO: BUST OF SAINT PAUL. GRANADA CATHEDRAL.

The same artist who created such a sensitive *Immaculate Conception* also carved this vigorous and virile head of St Paul. In its impressive naturalism and almost Olympic assurance it would seem to derive more from Donatello than Michelangelo, but such an affinity can only be coincidence, since Cano never went to Italy and he could only have known the work of these artists through engravings or drawings.

With Cano the subject matter of his works was never the pretext for a mere display of virtuosity, for he concentrated his inspiration in the interpretation of the spiritual content of his themes. The physical aspect of the apostle is far from ordinary: all the power and passion of his preaching is suggested in his solemn face with its thoughtful, sunken eyes, his furrowed brow and high forehead showing signs of premature baldness, and the way his long beard flows over his chest to the left as if he had just jerked his head round. The impression of sudden movement, given by the *contrapposto* in the bust, is one of vital energy poised between calm and violence.

The size of the head, somewhat larger than life, adds to the impressive effect of the work. Its power is strengthened by the polychromy, doubtless by Cano's own hand. The colours are light brown for the flesh parts, dark brown for the hair and beard, and violet-grey for the draperies.

The destination Cano had in mind for the bust is not known. All we do know is that it was acquired by Granada Cathedral in 1775 and that it had traditionally been attributed to Cano. It was first placed in a chapel and is now in the museum of the cathedral.

66 and 67. CANO AND MENA: SAINT JOSEPH WITH THE INFANT CHRIST. MUSEUM OF FINE ARTS, GRANADA.

It would seem probable that when Pedro de Mena executed the statues for the Convento del Ángel after models by Cano, his master gave him a progressively freer hand in each of them. We can accordingly take the statue of St Anthony to be the first that Mena carved, and that of St Joseph to be the last of the four, on the basis of its style which has features that were to be characteristic of Mena's work for the remainder of his career.

The *St Joseph* is a companion piece to the *St Anthony* which also has the Infant Christ in the saints' arms. The Infant is held only with the left arm for the right had to grasp the flowering staff. St Joseph is wearing a dark, wine-red tunic and a dark honey-coloured cloak. The only known version by Cano of this saint with the Child is a statuette found in Seville, and a signed canvas which is very similar, but both versions are substantially different from that here illustrated.

The statue lacks Cano's elegance and the folds of the draperies are more studied and irregular. The modelling of the hair and the flesh parts is more characteristic of Mena and suggests that in this instance he had followed his own inclinations in interpreting his master's model. Mena's subsequent versions of the same theme were very similar, and the treatment of the Child is so close to that in his *Virgin of Bethlehem* (now lost) for Santo Domingo, Málaga, that he would seem to have used the same model for both works. The Child is ugly, for He has a bulging forehead, small eyes, and a flattened nose, but the naturalism and liveliness of the figure is nonetheless charming. His right hand is vigorously clutching at St Joseph's tunic at the neck as though He were afraid of falling from His insecure position on the saint's arm and He is bent forward to look downwards, as is only natural considering the height at which the statue was placed.

When Pedro de Mena carved this statue he was still under Cano's influence and had not yet developed his more dramatic style, but his treatment of reality was inspired by his youthful optimism and the fact that he had recently become a father. It is highly likely that the Christ Child was modelled after one of the artist's little daughters for its appearance is too realistic for it to have been a product of his imagination alone. Mena was already showing a tendency towards the direct representation of reality, eliminating the elegant stylization that marks Cano's works.

68. CANO AND MENA: SAINT ANTHONY OF PADUA. MUSEUM OF FINE ARTS, GRANADA.

Pedro de Mena was twenty-four years old when Cano moved to Granada in 1652, and his father, Alonso de Mena, had the most important workshop in the city during the first half of the century. He died three years before Cano's return and left Pedro in charge, who promptly became a pupil of Cano's, working under the latter until his move to Madrid in 1656. When Cano finally came back to Granada for good in 1659, Mena was established at Málaga.

According to a tradition which is repeated by Palomino, it was Mena who made the four large statues for the transept of the Convento del Ángel at Granada, which was Cano's chief architectural work. Mena worked in the church under Cano who provided the models for the statues. This statement by Palomino is borne out by examination of the statues which have the stylistic characteristics of both sculptors. They are all Canoesque in character but only two, the *St Anthony* and the *St Diego,* are executed in Cano's usual manner, the *St Joseph* and the *St Peter of Alcantarà* show more evidence of Mena's hand. They are somewhat larger than life-size and are painted with oils over a primed surface as in easel-paintings. This was Cano's habitual technique and, according to Palomino again, it was he who painted the figures. Both the church and the convent were destroyed by the French during the Napoleonic occupation but the statues were preserved by the municipal authorities until they were finally acquired, a few years ago, by the museum.

Cano's style is best revealed in the statue of St Anthony of Padua. It is a full-length representation of the saint as a young man, holding the naked Christ Child in his arms. The realism of the figure has been softened by a tendency towards idealization, and Cano's characteristic good taste. He had already carved two other small images of St Anthony, and the one in the church of San Nicolás at Murcia is signed by him, but neither version resembles that illustrated here. It seems certain that Mena was working after a model by Cano who himself shared in the carving, especially of the head, with its restrained modelling and typical expression, its oval face, pointed chin, and large almond-shaped eyes which are slightly raised at the corners. The plump and highly realistic Child is also typical of the master's style.

69 and 70. PEDRO DE MENA: MARY MAGDALENE. NATIONAL MUSEUM OF SCULPTURE, VALLADOLID.

Pedro de Mena carved this statue for the Jesuit Congregation of San Felipe Neri at Madrid. Following the dissolution of the order in the eighteenth century the statue was removed to the Convent of the Visitation at Salesas. In 1919 it was acquired by the Prado Museum which loaned it to the museum at Valladolid when it was reorganised in 1933; it has remained there ever since as the sole representative of Andalusian sculpture.

The *Magdalene* is slightly less than life-size and is finely carved in cedar-wood, which was the usual material for choice works, and has an inscription on its base which reads "Petrus D. Mena I Medrano Granatensis Malaca Faciebat Anno 1664", proving the name of the artist, his provenance, the date and place of its execution.

The theme of the work has no precedent in Andalusian sculpture, although some examples are to be found in Castile. Apart from a *Magdalene* in the church of San Miguel, Valladolid, attributed without sufficient foundation to Gregorio Fernández, there is another version in the Descalzas Reales at Madrid, which antedates Mena's work and is undoubtedly Castilian. Other examples have been found in Galicia, Asturias and Castile and show that the theme had been diffused, but little light can be thrown on their origins since they are undated. In Andalusia, however, not even Mena's statue found any imitators. It was carved at Málaga where he had his work-shop but he had been to Madrid and it is there that he was probably inspired by some Castilian *Magdalene,* either by Fernández or by one of his school.

Like nearly all Andalusians, Mena was not an openly dramatic sculptor. He differed from Cano, who sought to beautify reality by idealizing it, by expressing emotion through an un-idealized naturalism. He brought out the repressed anguish and the fervour of the inner life of his saints and penitents, his Dying Christs and his Dolorosas. Far from being rhetorical, his *Magdalene* is notably restrained in her expression. Her emaciated face still bears traces of great beauty but her body is without the least hint of sensuality, being swathed in a dress of palm matting that conceals her figure completely. Her head, hands and feet are carved with outstanding mastery, but no detail is exaggerated, although Mena display his virtuosity in the carving of the hair, which hangs in long lank strands down her body. Even the little crucifix held in her left hand is a masterpiece in its own right.

Mena's *Magdalene* was one of the most popular images of its time and it was profusely imitated all over Castile. Among the best copies it inspired are the one in the church of San Antón, Madrid, and another, now lost, which belonged to the Magdalen convent at Alcalá de Henares. Another of Mena's works in the Museum at Valladolid is the beautiful Maria Aegyptica, which some scholars have attributed — in my opinion wrongly — to Juan Pascal de Mena.

71 and 72. PEDRO DE MENA: SAINT PETER OF ALCANTARÁ. GÜELL COLLECTION, BARCELONA.

St Peter of Alcantará was a comparatively recent saint who became the object of popular devotion in the seventeenth century, together with SS Teresa and Juan de Dios and the Jesuit saints. He was renowned as a great ascetic and Franciscan reformer, being greatly venerated by St Teresa who said "he seemed to be made of roots". He was represented several times by Pedro de Mena whose versions found numerous imitators. His first was made for the Convento del Ángel and, like its companion figures, under the direction of Cano who provided the models. Of the four, it is the least influenced by Cano, even though it was not typical of Mena's later style. Mena set the pattern for all his subsequent representations of the saint with his statue for the convent of San Antonio Abad at Granada – a beautiful piece of sculpture executed in a spirit of sober realism. It was then copied with only slight variations, especially in statuette form which was very popular in Granada, and became diffused throughout Spain.

The statue illustrated is one of the best of the series and is undoubtedly by Mena's hand. It formerly belonged to the Marquesa de Villadarias at Madrid before passing into the Güel Collection at Barcelona. It is a small figure, only 33 ½ inches high, similar in type and attitude to the figure of *St Anthony*, but more refined and stylized in its execution, as though to heighten its inner spirit. The saint stands erect, without the classical stoop that was favoured by Montañés and Cano. The slenderness of the figure is emphasized by the thick symmetrical folds in the habit which are arranged almost schematically, falling vertically without revealing the lines of the body. Despite the austere treatment of the draperies the body beneath them seems really to exist and the bare feet are visible, the left foot being slightly advanced. The slender, nervous hands are marvellously carved, but their position seems strange without the book and the pen they once held.

Certainly, the head is the most interesting part of the statue: in its emaciation it seems to be almost fleshless with the skull showing under the skin as though the saint were mummified, and so it might well be, were it not for the expression in the eyes. Not old age but mortification of the flesh has enabled the figure to shed his fleshly covering as though to release the spirit it contained.

When Mena carved this figure he was at the height of his artistic powers. His carving had become purer, his treatment more sober, and he had been able to round off the slightest detail without it distracting from the basic form. Later on his restraint was to degenerate into insipidity and plastic poverty, and his expressive power into a weak sentimentality. This decline can be seen in his later versions, from the *St Peter of Alcantará* in the museum of Barcelona (formerly in a private collection at Málaga) which shows the figure lifting his mantle, to the statue of *St Francis* in Cordoba, which is cold and overdone. There are also numerous imitations and workship copies.

73. JOSÉ DE MORA: THE VIRGIN DOLOROSA. CONVENTO DE ZAFRA, GRANADA.

After Mena, José de Mora was the most important sculptor at Granada. He was born of a family of sculptors and had the art in his blood. Since his childhood he had known Cano in his father Bernardo's workshop. Bernardo de Mora had directed the workshop after Mena had left for Málaga, and it was there that Cano worked, since he had none of his own. José de Mora was twenty-five when Cano died in 1667 and was profoundly influenced by him, much more than by Mena, or his own father who was a mediocre sculptor. In 1669 he went to Madrid where he worked with another of Cano's pupils, Sebastián de Herrera Barnuevo. In 1672 he was appointed Royal Sculptor to Carlos II, but relinquished the post when he settled permanently at Granada in 1680 after working in both cities at various times.

The companion busts of the *Ecce Homo* and the *Dolorosa* are among the most remarkable works produced by a Granadine sculptor. Like the statuettes that were so popular at Granada, the busts were intended for worship in the home or a convent. Busts of the *Ecce Homo* had already been made at Seville and Granada – and one has even been attributed to Cano – but it was Mena who seems to have carved the *Dolorosa* bust, establishing it as a companion piece for the *Ecce Homo*. Mora took over the theme but preferred the smaller proportion of the bust-form busts to Mena's half-length figures with hands showing, in order to concentrate the spectator's attention on the face alone. He always carved pairs, but he found the *Dolorosa* more suited to the expression of his soft and almost feminine sensibility. This *Dolorosa* formed a pair with a bust of the *Ecce Homo*. Whereas it is one of the finest of the series, the second work was inferior and had a very different expressive content. Unlike the version in the church of Santa Ana, the Virgin is wearing neither head-dress nor hood; her tunic falls below the neck and her hair can be seen under the mantle over her head. Mora's modelling has become extraordinarily pure and by using a file he has managed to obtain the utmost smoothness and delicacy of execution. The eyebrows are raised to express sorrow in a way that was to become characteristic. The Virgin's downcast eyes and tremulous looking mouth that seems to be containing her grief made it unnecessary for the artist to add tears to her face to complete the effect. Her youth is emphasized by her shapely neck, the perfect oval of her face and her long hair. Rather than the Mother grieving over the death of her Son, she could be the Virgin suddenly foreseeing the suffering that the Child in her arms would have to undergo in the future. The polychromy is as smooth and delicate as the carving. The colours are rose-pink for the tunic, blue for the mantle, both having borders embellished with gold arabesques, and a matt light brown for the flesh parts with a very dark brown for the hair.

74 and 75. JOSÉ DE MORA: VIRGIN OF SORROWS. CHURCH OF SANTA ANA, GRANADA.

According to its archives, the Congregation of San Felipe Neri contracted Mora to carve a *Virgin of Sorrows* when he was in Granada in 1671. He completed the work six months later, and it was carried in procession into the church accompanied by a crowd of fervent worshippers. When the Congregation was dissolved in 1834 the statue was removed to its present location in Santa Ana where it has continued to be the object of uninterrupted popular devotion.

The *Virgin's* costume is the same as that in Gaspar Becerra's work for Queen Isabel of Valois and could have been seen by Mora in Madrid. According to tradition however, Mora based his statue on the version painted by Cano. The *Virgin* is shown kneeling, her hands clasped in an attitude of prayer, her head inclined and her eyes turned downwards. She is wearing the customary dress for widows, which was inspired by Queen Joan's mourning costume on the death of her husband, Philip the Handsome: a white tunic, a coif with head-dress, and a long black cloak covering the head. The costume is identical to that in Mazo and Carreno's portraits of Philip IV's widow, Queen Mariana, and was to become conventional in representations of the *Soledad*. Mora's *Virgin* conforms to the model that had been established but the original position of the hands has been changed. When the statue was taken to its first site they were joined together and covered the face; Mora accordingly decided to alter them by placing them crossed over the bosom, which was done in 1707, probably by his own hand. Even though the model for the figure was not of his own devising, his interpretation of the theme is completely individualistic. The interest of the works is not in its costume but in its carving and delicately expressed emotion, which was never to be surpassed either by Mora himself or by any other sculptor.

It is a youthful work but nonetheless perfect in every detail. If we compare it with similar figures by Juní or Gregorio Fernández, it will strike us not as the result of an opposed personal sensibility on Mora's part, but rather as the expression of a radically different artistic conception. The grief of the Castilian Dolorosas is violent: their attitudes and gestures are rhetorical as though they were beseeching heaven and earth to take part in their suffering. Mora's *Virgin* keeps her anguish to herself, hiding it within her bosom and under her downcast eyelids. Her sorrow is deeper, more intimate, quietist: it is only revealed by her tears as they fall silently down her calm face which is almost frozen in its impassivity. The Virgin is not so much grieving as *suffering* with that peculiarly Andalusian intensity of feeling, which is capable of killing while yet remaining undetected.

Mora is the most subtly sensitive of all the Granadine sculptors. He had neither Cano's powerful imagination, nor Mena's realism, but his strength lay in the concentration of all the mystical outpouring of his lonely, restless spirit into a delicate, deeply rooted expression of emotion. He was never a painter but he had learned polychromy from Cano and was able to combine form and colour harmoniously, following his inspiration and his own, very individual, concepts.

76 and 77. JOSÉ DE MORA: SAINT PANTALEON. CHURCH OF SANTA ANA, GRANADA.

St Pantaleon, the saintly physician from Nicolemia who was martyred in the reign of Diocletian, is one of the patron saints of doctors, together with SS Cosmos and Damian. His statue was made by Mora for the medical and surgical guild at Granada, but its date is unknown.

After his wife had died childless, Mora's eccentricities of character became more pronounced and he eventually went insane. In his final period he secluded himself in his house at Albayzín (built by the poet Soto de Rojas for his own pleasure) and only worked at night for fear of being observed; it was under these conditions that Palomino saw him in 1712, the year of his last works. His gentle, harmless insanity made him cease work and he died in 1724 at the age of eighty-two.

Mora's *St Pantaleon* was almost certainly one of his last works for it bears a strong stylistic resemblance to his figures for the Charterhouse at Granada. It is an unusual statue and the modelling is both summary and superficial as though it were a sketch. Its effect is rather that of a painting, for the colour of the whole composition takes precedence over the form. Obsessed as he was with the Dolorosa theme, Mora gave his statue the same features as those of the *Virgin* in the Convent of Santa Isabel. The face is inclined towards the crucifix held in the left hand and has an expression of affliction, but whether this is due to the death of Christ or the saint's impending martyrdom it is hard to say. The modelling of the face and hands is summary and almost schematic; the matt pallor of the flesh parts is heightened by the blackness of the hair, and the throat bears the red trace of a sword wound, but we do not know if the saint is meant to be alive or not. The polychromy is a soft, dark wine-red for the tunic, black for the long gown which is open at the front, and white, the only light tone, for the cuffs and collar. The figure has an attitude of drooping languor which is accentuated by the way the hand is held against the chest, stressing the extreme youth of the saint.

This is certainly a strange way of depicting a physician and, what is more, a martyr. Mora seems incapable of freeing himself from his obsession with languid, suffering figures that personified his own morbid melancholia. The theme mattered little to him in this statue for it was his own soul he was depicting.

78. JOSÉ DE MORA: SAINT BRUNO. SACRISTY OF THE CHARTERHOUSE, GRANADA.

The style of this small statue of St Bruno resembles that of the many versions made by Cano and Mena, but the theme was an unusual one for Mora. He carved another image of the saint together with his other figures for the sanctuary in the same Charterhouse, but this was a much larger work influenced by Pereyra's version for the portal of the San Paular hospice in Madrid. It was made in about 1712 shortly before his madness, which had already become evident, forced him to stop working.

The smaller *St Bruno* standing in the capitular hall is certainly the earlier of the two versions, for it has a balance of line and a richness of modelling that Mora was to lose in his later work. Because of its artistic excellence rather than its style it has been attributed to Cano, in contradiction to Palomino's conclusive statement, made after he had been painting in the Charterhouse in 1712 in close contact with Mora, who was carving the statues for the sanctuary.

It has been said of Pereyra's *St Bruno* at Miraflores that the only reason it did not speak was because it was a Carthusian. The same cannot be said for Mora's statue, for its silence is so eloquent that it seems to be sending up a mystical oration from the half-open mouth and ecstatic eyes. The saint's arms are clasped over his bosom as if to prevent his soul from soaring heavenwards together with his prayers. Mora's work was conceived in a sudden fit of artistic inspiration and reached heights of mysticism never before attained by sculpture. The figure is not expressing the spirit of asceticism or penitence, nor the energy of one who has founded a great religious order, but only an intensity of passion that seems to consume the whole body in a blaze of supernatural love.

The carving is perfect. The folds of the drapery are arranged in smooth lines with rich *chiaroscuro* effects, and fabric dipped in glue has been used for the most detailed parts. The habit was gilded before the paint was applied, giving the white a warm glow. The delicately modelled head and the expressive, tremulous hands are painted a pale matt brown. The statue can be dated about 1707 by the way the hands are crossed over the chest, for this was the year when the hands of Mora's *Dolorosa* were altered to the same position, almost certainly by the artist himself.

79 and 80: FRANCISCO DE RIBAS: INFANT CHRIST. SAN JUAN DE LA PALMA, SEVILLE.

The existence of the brothers Felipe, Francisco, and Gaspar de Ribas has only recently been brought to light by documentary evidence. Previously only the name of Gaspar was known, as he was mentioned by Ceán as one of Montañés's pupils, but now we know that they all came from Cordoba and are familiar with many of their works. Felipe had worked with Cano and died prematurely in 1648, when his work was continued by his brother Francisco, who was documented until 1679, the date of his will. Like Felipe, Francisco enthusiastically adopted the Baroque style in his use of restless gestures, flying draperies and thick, turbulent masses of hair for his figures.

Francisco de Ribas gave his *Infant Christ* to the Sevillian parish church of San Juan de la Palma in 1644. As the church did not have to pay for the sculpture, it took great pains with the polychromy for the statue which was the work of Gaspar de Ribas, who embellished it with gilt and jewels set in the ornamentation of the tunic.

The Infant Christ was a favourite subject for free-standing devotional images in Spain during the seventeenth and eighteenth centuries. Others were made in the sixteenth century, including one by Bautista Vázquez. The model was established by Montañés with his image for the Confraternity of the Sanctuary at Seville, which he carved in the nude since it was to be adorned with real costumes. Such naked Infant Christs were widely popular throughout Andalusia: they were either carved or cast in lead or calamine and always showed the figure in full-length in the act of benediction with a crucifix in the left hand. They appealed to a certain form of sentimental piety, particularly in women, which explains why they are so often found in convents, especially as they were images which had to be costumed.

By way of contrast, the whole figure of the Child by Ribas is carved. He is wearing a wide-sleeved tunic ending well below the neck and above the forearms, and opening at one side to reveal the left leg as was conventional in Baroque representations of angels. The base consists of a cloud filled with cherub's heads, as in traditional statues of the *Immaculate Conception*. The whole composition has a Baroque wind-swept quality with its billowing draperies, swirling hair, sense of restless movement and instability that so appealed to artists of the time, even though it was a contradiction of the very essence of sculptural form. Ribas definitely managed to preserve a certain sense of balance and avoided the frivolity that typified eighteenth-century art. The graceful features of the Child have a grave expression as though He had suddenly received a premonition of His divinely tragic destiny.

The statue is an early forerunner of the movement towards full Baroque that was led in Seville by Alonso Cano's pupils and followers.

81-88. PEDRO ROLDÁN: BURIAL OF CHRIST. HOSPITAL DE LA CARIDAD, SEVILLE.

The Sevillian hospital of La Caridad is one of the artistic treasure-houses of seventeenth-century art, even though many of its paintings were removed by Marshal Soult during the French occupation. The story of its foundation is well known: the nobleman Don Miguel de Mañara repented of his dissipated youth and decided to devote the rest of his life and his worldly goods to relieving the poor. He re-organized the ancient Brotherhood of the Santa Caridad and built a new and magnificent hospital. The chapel was decorated with paintings by Murillo and Valdés Leal and a great sculptural altar, all having as themes Christ's Holy Works.

In its magnificent design and its harmony of architecture, sculpture, and painting the altar is the masterpiece of Spanish Baroque art. The Brotherhood expressed their wish that the sacred image of the Dead Christ should be given "the finest sepulchre that it is in our power to create" and commissioned

the architect of the church, Bernardo Simon de Pineda, for the design, Pedro Roldán for the carving, and Valdés Leal for the polychromy. With its Salomonic columns and sumptuous vegetal decorations the altar served as a splendid framework for the sculpted *Burial of Christ*. The figures are larger than life, entirely carved in the round, and are placed against a relief of the *Calvary*, complete with the two thieves on their crosses. To complete the imagery, the altar is flanked with statues of SS George and Roch and crowned with the three Theological Virtues.

Pedro Roldán is the last of the great Sevillian sculptors of the seventeenth century. He was born in Seville in 1624, grew up at Antequera, which he always regarded as his home town, and trained at Granada under Alonso de Mena, moving on to Seville after the latter's death. His works show the influence of Mena and the Granadine school, but not of Cano, who only arrived after he had left Granada. When Roldán came to Seville, Montañés was already dead and had been succeeded by second-rate imitators or pupils of Cano. Roldán soon stood out among his fellow sculptors and eventually was regarded as the foremost in the city, which explains why he was chosen to do the altar carvings in La Caridad.

In its composition Roldán's *Burial of Christ* may have been influenced by his memories of Jacopo Florentino's version at Granada, but nothing could illustrate better the differences between the two works than the Baroque exuberance of the one in contrast to the Renaissance balance of the other. The positions of the figures have changed as well: instead of simply holding the ends of the sheet under the body of Christ, both Joseph of Arimathea and Nicodemus are seizing it violently and one of them has thrown himself down to kiss Christ's feet. Roldán has given both personages elaborate and rather fanciful Oriental costumes. The group behind the bier consists of the Virgin, Saint John, the Magdalene and two other women, one of whom is almost hidden behind Joseph. On the right two youths hold up the stone slab from the entrance of the tomb.

Roldán departed from tradition in his rendering of the figures. There is very little to distinguish the four women from one another: they all wear mantles and hoods and only the Virgin is easily recognizable from her central position and posture with hands crossed on her bosom and face turned upwards as in all conventional representations of the *Dolorosa*. The

Magdalene is the other outstanding female figure by her beauty and careful carving. Roldán's St John is shown bearded instead of as the conventionally clean-shaven youth, but this departure from the usual model was already begun by Pablo de Rojas and was adopted by Montañés.

The effect of the composition is rather one of movement than dramatic emotion. The characterization of the figures has a certain monotony and their expressions are not deeply felt. Roldán's sculpture is lightly executed and full of movement but also superficial, and the emotion aroused by the work is due more to the over-all composition than to the life of any one figure. The technique of the carving shows a considerable change, for the work is chiselled in large planes without being toned down with a file, and the hair and draperies of the figures have been executed in heavy compact masses. There is not a single straight line in the work, neither in the attitudes of the figures nor the draperies: it is full of gently flowing curves which contribute to the feeling of restless movement.

After the realism of the preceding period, stylization returned again to sculpture. The Renaissance paid homage to beauty by idealising reality; Baroque artists simplified form and chose movement to express inner life. This tendency towards synthetic form can be clearly seen in Roldán's work. He was the typical sculptor of the time, before sculpture was dominated by painting and was made to reproduce its effects.

The polychromy plays a vital part in the altarpiece. Valdés Leal was usually an impetuous artist who improvised as he worked, but for his work in the hospital he brought a discipline to his striving for perfection that was quite alien to his temperament. It can be seen in his great paintings of the *Death of Christ* and particularly in the beautifully executed polychromy of the altar. His soft harmonious colours and gilded tones enhanced Roldán's forms and made them vibrate with movement. The landscape in the background is carved in low relief and its painterly effect adds considerable depth to the composition.

Roldán's death in 1699 preceded that of the last Hapsburg king of Spain by only a few months, and with him the great age of Sevillian sculpture came to its end.

PRINTED IN SWITZERLAND